JOHN, JESUS, AND THE RENEWAL OF ISRAEL

John, Jesus, and the Renewal of Israel

Richard Horsley *&* Tom Thatcher

WILLIAM B. EERDMANS PUBLISHING COMPANY

GRAND RAPIDS, MICHIGAN / CAMBRIDGE, U.K.

Published 2013 by
Wm. B. Eerdmans Publishing Co.
2140 Oak Industrial Drive N.E., Grand Rapids, Michigan 49505 /
P.O. Box 163, Cambridge CB3 9PU U.K.

Printed in the United States of America

18 17 16 15 14 13   7 6 5 4 3 2 1

Library of Congress Cataloging-in-Publication Data

Horsley, Richard A.
John, Jesus, and the renewal of Israel / Richard Horsley & Tom Thatcher.
pages   cm
Includes bibliographical references and index.
ISBN 978-0-8028-6872-5 (pbk.: alk. paper)
1. Bible. John — Criticism, interpretation, etc.
2. Jews — History — 168 B.C.-135 A.D.
I. Thatcher, Tom, 1967-   II. Title.

BS2615.52.H67   2013

226.5′06 — dc23

2013010384

www.eerdmans.com

Contents

———◦◦◦———

v

CONTENTS

Reclaiming John as a Source for Jesus

T he title of this book, *John, Jesus, and the Renewal of Israel,* indicates both its focus and its thesis. We offer a new reading of the Gospel of John as a story of Jesus' mission in the historical context of early Roman Palestine. We will argue that the Gospel of John portrays Jesus engaged in a renewal of the people of Israel against the rulers of Israel, both the Jerusalem authorities and the Romans who placed them in power.

This book began in a conversation about the potential value of the Gospel of John as a source for the historical Jesus. We share a conviction that the relationships between John, the other Gospels, and the historical Jesus need to be rethought in the light of recent research. For some time interpreters have assumed that the Gospel of John sheds light on the history of Johannine Christianity and the development of early Christian theology but very little light on the historical Jesus. For access to the historical Jesus, interpreters focus mainly or exclusively on the Synoptic Gospels or, more specifically, the Synoptic tradition. We believe that this sharp distinction between John and the Synoptic Gospels is based on an essential misunderstanding of the Gospels as ancient texts. A more appropriate understanding of the Gospels and of how any of them can serve as sources for the historical Jesus will require a substantial reconsideration of many standard assumptions, analyses, and approaches that have guided New Testament studies — many more, in fact, than we could possibly address here. For this project, therefore, we have narrowed the focus to John's portrayal of Jesus' mission.

Leaving the Old Paths

Even with the focus narrowed to John's portrayal of Jesus' mission, our project is complex, for at least two reasons. First, because interpretation of John's Gospel has focused on its unique Christological vision, there is little previous interpretation of the historical dimension of John's portrayal of Jesus to build upon, compared with the more extensive analysis of Mark's or Matthew's or Luke's portrayals. Second, our project is further complicated, as all future investigation and interpretation of Jesus must be, by a growing body of research on the historical context, the Gospels as narratives, and the ancient communications context in which the Gospel of John and all other sources for Jesus were produced.

The Gospel of John has long been viewed as very different from the Gospels of Matthew, Mark, and Luke, often called the "Synoptics" just because they appear to follow the same synopsis of Jesus' mission — a synopsis that John notably does not follow. John includes material not present in the Synoptics and lacks much of what they include. Thus, while the Fourth Gospel includes some of the best-known episodes in the Bible — water turned into wine, the woman at the well, sayings such as John 3:16 ("For God so loved the world . . .") and "I am the way, the truth, and the life" — John also ignores Synoptic scenes such as the Transfiguration and Peter's confession that Jesus is the "Christ" and includes no parables and no exorcisms. Not only in individual scenes and details but even in the very structure of the story, John follows his own course: while Mark suggests that Jesus moved around Galilee and its environs for about a year before traveling to Jerusalem to die almost immediately at the hands of the chief priests and Romans, John has Jesus moving back and forth from Galilee to Judea numerous times and all across both regions, including a trip through Samaria, over the course of a mission that must have covered at least three Passovers (John 2:13; 6:4; 13:1).

At first glance, one might think that the many differences between John and the Synoptics would make John a valuable source as an alternative portrayal of Jesus' mission. This has not been the case, however, largely because most interpreters today explain the distinctive elements of John's presentation by appealing to some version of a theory first proposed in the late second century by the theologian Clement of Alexandria. Clement thought that John, "knowing that the bodily things *(ta sōmatika)* had been manifested in the [other] Gospels . . . and being moved by God's Spirit, produced a spiritual Gospel (*pneumatikon euangelion;* Eusebius, *History of the Church* 6.14.5-7).[1] Two key features of Clement's theory remain foundational to most study of the Gospel of John today. First, John wrote last, and his book therefore represents a more advanced stage of theological reflection than do the Synoptics. Second, as a result of this advanced theological reflection, John's story promotes a more sophisticated or "higher" Christology than the Synoptics, "higher" meaning that John's outlook is "less Jewish" than what we see elsewhere in the New Testament and more in line with Hellenistic philosophical ideas that move well beyond what Jesus himself would have articulated.

Leaving aside the obvious question of why a "Jewish" outlook would be considered "lower" than a more Western outlook, it is simply the case that Clement's explanation of the difference between John and the Synoptic Gospels fails to account for much of the content in the "last" Gospel. While John's story does contain a good deal of reflective dialogue and discourse that the other Gospels do not, it also says quite a bit about Jesus' travels, his interactions with people, and especially the conflicts into which he came, particularly in Jerusalem. A critical reading of the Gospel of John must account for the whole Gospel, the seemingly more mundane aspects as well as the seemingly more "spiritual." Inasmuch as other scholars have said a great deal about the spiritual/theological side of John's presentation, our focus on John's portrayal of Jesus' mission may be taken as a supplement to the larger body of prior interpretation.

Insofar as we attempt to deal with the mundane features as well as the "spiritual" aspects of the Fourth Gospel, we will not follow some pre-

---

1. Translation by Thatcher, based on the Greek text in the Loeb edition, Eusebius, *The Ecclesiastical History,* trans. Kirsopp Lake and J. E. L. Oulton (Cambridge: Harvard University Press, 1953).

vious paths of interpretation. We will not treat John's Gospel as a book of theology, particularly Christology. Nor will we treat the Gospel of John as a potential source for tidbits of information about the historical Jesus, isolating individual elements of John's presentation, ranking them on a scale of historical "authenticity," and determining whether they are more or less historical than data from the Synoptics. Nor will we treat the Gospel of John as a redacted text or a text that tells primarily the story of its own composition history. All this has already been done by other scholars, and without commenting on their methods and conclusions we simply wish to clarify that we are not following that track here. We will instead treat the Gospel as a coherent narrative derived from a formative community memory that includes differing strands that have been brought together.

Exploring a New Path

In pursuing a new path to what the Gospels might tell us about Jesus, our approach will be informed by recent research and approaches that fall outside the traditional scope of studies of Jesus and the Gospels. Like many academic fields, New Testament studies has become highly specialized, with the result that it is difficult for experts in one area of research to keep up with developments in other areas. Specialists in exegesis of the Gospels and the interpretation of Jesus have continued to refine the philological and form-critical analysis of Greek terms, Gospel verses and pericopes, and Jesus' sayings and Jesus-stories. In the last several decades, however, other scholars have carried out new research in several areas that bear directly on our understanding both of the Gospels as sources and of the historical context of Jesus' life, new research that most Jesus scholars are just now beginning to consider. Three general areas of research have come together in our discussions and are foundational for the approach we are exploring.

First, beginning in the 1970s an increasing number of Gospel interpreters began to recognize that the Gospels are stories. A surge of "narrative-critical" studies in the 1980s applied principles of modern literary criticism to these ancient texts, with attention (for example) to the communication between implied authors and implied readers, plot and character development, and stylistic devices like irony. Most important, and most distinguishing this line of research from prior study, was the basic recognition that the Gospels are *stories,* sustained connected narratives with overarching themes and purposes, not just collections of sayings, episodes, and Christological statements. More recently it has been recognized that the Gospels are different from modern fiction. They are ancient stories and, more important, historical stories. No matter how much we may question their reliability, the Gospels are historical stories about a Galilean villager who was acclaimed as a prophet and/or anointed one, who interacted with Galilean and other peasants of Israelite heritage, whose followers formed a movement in early Roman Palestine, and who was crucified by the Roman governor of Judea. To be understood appropriately, the Gospels must be read in historical context.

Second, more recently, and partly stimulated by the recognition of the Gospels as narratives, a small number of New Testament scholars have begun to research the larger communications context of antiquity, the media culture in which stories about Jesus were produced and published. In John's world, literacy was limited, communications were predominantly oral, and culture was cultivated through social memory. Exploration of the implications of such research for biblical studies, which is solidly embedded in modern print-culture, is only just beginning. Our discussion here is informed by what has come to light so far, in full awareness that media studies are still in a state of infancy.

Third, preceding and developing alongside this growing recognition of the Gospels as historical stories and research into ancient communications media has been an ever more comprehensive and precise investigation of the general history (not just the religious history) of Roman Palestine. Stimulated by such factors as the publication of the Dead Sea Scrolls, more historically critical approaches to archaeology, and attention to modern anticolonial movements, historians have attended more broadly and carefully to social, political, and economic issues. Biblical and Jewish historians have begun to ask questions and apply approaches borrowed from their "secular" counterparts and from social anthropologists. As the result of this expansion and precision of knowledge of ancient Palestine in the context of the Roman Empire, it is clear that the context of Jesus and the Gospels involved social-political conflicts, regional differences, and a diversity of movements. This was the historical context in which Jesus operated and from which the Gospels originated.

This more comprehensive and precise attention to the historical context in which Jesus and the Gospels belonged is leading to the dawning recognition that some of the most basic concepts of New Testament studies are seriously problematic. New Testament studies, a division of modern theology, developed on the basis of modern Western culture, in which religion was assumed to be separate from political-economic life — indeed, where religion was reduced to individual belief. Jesus and the Gospels were, almost by definition, viewed as religious and not political. In the ancient world, however, religion was inseparable from political-economic life. The Roman emperor was honored as a "son of god" in temples and shrines. The Jerusalem temple was the ruling political-economic institution in ancient Judea as well as the holy place where priests offered sacrifices to God. The "Lord's Prayer" that Jesus taught his followers appealed for the political-religious rule of God as well as sufficient food and cancellation of debts. The Gospels, like "the Law and the Prophets," are about all of life, life that is inseparably political-economic-religious.

Modern synthetic concepts such as "(early) Judaism" and "(early) Christianity" are thus problematic in two major respects. First, they obscure the actual larger or smaller political-economic-religious formations such as village communities and the Jerusalem temple-state and Herodian courts and popular movements and nascent communities to which the sources refer, as well as the power-relations among them. Indeed, second, it should now be evident that at the time of Jesus and the Gospels what is referred to as (early) Judaism and what is referred to as (early) Christianity did not yet exist, but emerged only gradually under the Roman Empire in late antiquity as identifiable diverse religious communities and practices.

We are convinced that interpretation of the Gospels and of Jesus must attend to the implications of recent research in all the areas mentioned above. Complicating our efforts to do so is the simple fact that explorations in these relatively new areas of literary analysis, media studies, and historical studies have often proceeded separately. Like others whose work has cut across several of these new areas, however, we sense the mutually reinforcing implications of all of these initiatives for rethinking interpretation of the Gospels.

Four Steps

In attempting to bring these lines of research together in investigation of the Gospel of John and its portrayal of Jesus' mission, we will proceed in four steps of two chapters each.

The first step provides a basis for understanding the story of John in its historical context. In chapter one we sketch the fundamental political-economic-religious structure and dynamics of Roman Palestine, including the cultural divide corresponding to the fundamental divide between the ruling elite and the ordinary people. Compounding that divide were the historical regional differences mitigated by shared Israelite tradition, which we outline in chapter two.

In the second step, chapter three begins with the recognition that the Gospels are historical stories and that these stories, not individual sayings, are the sources for interpretation of Jesus. Accordingly, we then present a summary literary analysis of Mark's story and the sequence of the speeches in "Q," thought to be the earliest Gospel texts and those most studied to date, and sketch their respective portrayals of Jesus. In chapter four the necessity of taking the Gospels as whole stories as the sources for Jesus is reinforced by taking into account various lines of investigation into ancient communications media.

In the third step, building on the indications and implications of the previous chapters, we focus on the Gospel of John as a story about Jesus' mission. In chapter five, taking some cues from the previous analysis of Mark's story and the Q speeches, we first investigate the Gospel of John as a story, with attention to setting, characters, and plot, and then summarize the Gospel's portrayal of Jesus and his mission. In the sixth chapter, we then note the fundamental ways in which John's story fits, at least in broad terms, the historical context outlined in step two.

Finally, in the fourth step, building on the previous three but particularly on chapter five, we explore the fuller portrayal of Jesus in John's story, presenting Jesus' mission as the generation of a renewal of Israel, in chapter seven, in opposition to and by the rulers of Israel, in chapter eight.

Only in the Epilogue, in a somewhat tentative and speculative way, will we venture to point out some of the implications of the investigation for using John's story and portrayal of Jesus' mission as a source for the historical Jesus and return to consider the relation of the more "spiritual" aspects of the story to the more "mundane" renewal of Israel against the rulers.

Before proceeding, it is relevant to offer two important caveats and several words of appreciation. First, we wish to stress that what we are presenting here is no more than a provisional sketch — necessarily so, since we and others are only just beginning to sense the implications of heretofore separate lines of recent research and their challenges to standard assumptions, approaches, and concepts in New Testament studies. It seems inappropriate, almost beside the point, to compare our reading of John with others that proceed from different assumptions and that utilize different analytical methods. This leads to a second caveat: we will only rarely engage in discussion with important studies on the Gospel of John and the historical Jesus, even those for which we have high regard, in either the text or the notes. We realize that we are pursuing a provisional exploration and want to keep the presentation as simple and manageable as possible, and we specifically do not wish to imply that other approaches must be wrong in order for ours to be right.

Finally, we would like to express special appreciation and gratitude to several colleagues who have deeply influenced our work. Werner Kelber, who pioneered investigation of orality and literacy, of Gospel narrative, and of cultural memory in New Testament studies, has been our principal mentor in all those areas. At Werner's invitation(s), the late John Miles Foley, perhaps the foremost theorist of oral performance who worked across several academic fields, generously contributed to programs of the Society of Biblical Literature (SBL) and a number of international conferences on orality and literacy. His wide-ranging crosscultural knowledge of oral lore and sensitive critical interdisciplinary theoretical reflection are becoming increasingly influential in study of the Gospels. Correspondingly, the political-anthropological research, wide cross-cultural knowledge, and social-political theory of James C. Scott, who has also generously participated in sessions of the SBL, are becoming increasingly influential in our understanding of the movements Jesus generated and the Gospel stories they produced. And Barry Schwartz, pioneer in the interdisciplinary analysis of social memory, has generously participated in SBL programs where he has mentored some of us who are just beginning to explore social memory as a prominent factor in the texts on which we focus, such as the Gospel of John. We thank all of them for leaving footprints big enough for so many of us to walk in.

The Historical Context of the Gospels and Jesus

CHAPTER ONE

Division in Roman Palestine

Since the Gospel of John, like the other canonical Gospels, is not just a story but a historical story, one that refers to and incorporates elements of the actual past, we begin with a sketch of the historical context from which it emerged and which it claims to describe. So that the procedure is not circular, we construct this sketch of the political-economic-religious structure and dynamics of Roman Palestine at the time of Jesus from sources other than the Gospels. We also purposely attempt to present the structural conflict and dynamics in Judea, Samaria, and Galilee as they appear in the extra-Gospel sources themselves and do not select incidents and issues that we think will illuminate particular features of the Gospel story. This procedure sets up the possibility that the Gospel of John or other Gospels do not fit the resulting sketch of the historical situation. But it also sets up the possibility of discovering that some patterns and portrayals in the Gospels do fit the historical situation in broad terms.

The field of biblical studies shares the modern Western assumption that religion is separate from politics and economics. In the United States this posture even has a constitutional basis in the separation of church and state. In this highly individualistic society, moreover, religion has been reduced almost to individual belief.[1] New Testament studies in

---

1. See especially the critical discussion in Talal Asad, *Genealogies of Religion* (Baltimore: Johns Hopkins University Press, 1993), chapter 1.

particular focuses mainly on the religious dimension of life, with the result that scholars have often assumed that at the time of Jesus the principal social division was between the religion of Judaism and the culture of Hellenism. Viewed in this framework, Jesus and Paul are interpreted as religious leaders who catalyzed the transition from one religion, Judaism, to its successor, Christianity. When the political dimension has been considered at all, discussion has been heavily influenced by "the Jewish revolt" of 66-73 CE, a complex sequence of events that is easily reduced to a conflict between "the Jews" and the pagan Romans and that is often conveniently summarized with reference to the singular event of "the Roman destruction of the temple" in Jerusalem.

Any adequate understanding of Jesus and the Gospels, however, must proceed from a recognition that religion, politics, and economics were inseparable in the ancient world. The Roman emperor, who ruled the Mediterranean world, was honored as a "son of god" in temples and shrines. The Jerusalem temple was the center of the economy in ancient Judea as well as the place where priests offered sacrifices to God. The Gospels, like the books of the Hebrew Bible, are about all of life, not just religion. Jesus' proclamation that "the kingdom of God is at hand" was a political as well as religious claim. In the prayer he taught his disciples, "Your will be done" means that all people would have sufficient food, cancellation of debts, and deliverance from being dragged into court on suspicion of subversion. In order to appreciate the import of the Gospels and understand the mission of Jesus it may be necessary to step outside the box of modern biblical studies.

Study of the Gospels and consideration of the historical Jesus have also been "boxed in" by broad, synthetic, essentialist concepts. Still today, textbooks tell us that Jesus and his followers were part of "Judaism," focused on the Temple and the Law, and that Judaism consisted primarily of four "sects," the Pharisees, the Sadducees, the Essenes, and the Zealots. As a "Jew" in the context of "Judaism," Jesus is discussed primarily in theological terms, such as how he reinterpreted or even opposed the Law in debates with the Pharisees.

One of the principal factors in the resurgence of interest in the historical Jesus was the more precise knowledge of his historical context that emerged in the 1970s and 1980s. The modern scholarly construct of "the Zealots," for example, had long blocked recognition of the variety of different movements among the ordinary people, as well as the different resistance groups among the scribal teachers.[2] Ironically, the most problematic of these scholarly constructs are also the most fundamental: "Judaism" and "Christianity." The most important sources for life in early Roman Palestine, including the histories of the wealthy Judean priest Josephus, the speeches of the earlier Judean scribe Jesus Ben Sira (second century BCE), the scribal *Psalms of Solomon* (first century BCE), and rabbinic debates echoed in the *Mishnah,* have no such concept as "Judaism." The Gospels of Mark, Matthew, and John have no concept of either "Judaism" or "Christianity." The Gospels not only understand Jesus and his followers as members of the people of Israel but evidently address communities that considered themselves to be within Israel. By imposing the later concepts of Judaism and Christianity onto our ancient sources, we block recognition of the diversity and dynamics of life in Judea and Galilee under Roman imperial rule.

Most basic for understanding the Gospels, including John, and for considering these texts as sources for the historical Jesus are the fundamental political-economic-religious structures and dynamics in Roman Palestine and the regional differences among Judea, Samaria, and Galilee. We will discuss the former in this chapter and the latter in the next, drawing on contemporary historical sources other than the Gospels, such as Josephus's histories, before focusing on the Gospels in the following chapters.

The Rulers, Their Retainers, and the Ruled

According to ancient Judean sources, the fundamental division in ancient Palestine under Roman rule was between the rulers, both the

---

2. The modern scholarly construct of "the Zealots," a composite of many different texts, protests, and movements, was elaborated most influentially by Martin Hengel, *Die Zeloten* (Leiden: Brill, 1961). For the emergence of the new perspective, see Morton Smith, "Zealots and Sicarii: Their Origins and Relations," *Harvard Theological Review* 64 (1971), 1-19, and the series of articles by Richard Horsley culminating in (with John Hanson) *Bandits, Prophets, and Messiahs: Popular Resistance Movements at the time of Jesus* (Minneapolis: Winston, 1985; Harrisburg: Trinity, 1999).

Romans and the local client rulers that they appointed, and the villagers they ruled. This division, moreover, was inseparably political-economic-religious.

This fundamental division between rulers and ruled, hidden by the concept "Judaism," was nothing new to the Roman era. In the accounts in 2 Samuel, for example, after the ancient Israelites had "anointed" ("messiahed") the young David as their king, he established centralized rule from Jerusalem, which he had captured with his mercenaries and tried to legitimate as the capital of Israel (2 Sam 2:2-5; 5:1-16; 6:1-15). The Israelites revolted twice, only to be beaten down by David's mercenaries (chs. 15–18 and 20). After the even more imperial king Solomon constructed his royal temple by imposing forced labor on the Israelites, the ten northern tribes again revolted and remained independent of Jerusalem rule for centuries (1 Kings 5, 11–12). Centuries later, the Persian imperial regime sponsored the establishment of a temple-state in Jerusalem headed by a priestly aristocracy (the "second temple"). Nehemiah, appointed governor of the fledgling society, had to set restraints on the aristocracy's exploitation of the people they ruled, stopping them from maneuvering villagers into debt and seizing their ancestral lands (Neh 5:1-10). The same fundamental political-economic-religious structure continued under Roman rule. Thanks mainly to the extensive histories composed by Josephus some sixty years after Jesus' death, we have far more extensive knowledge of the structure and dynamics of life in Palestine at the end of the second temple period.[3]

---

3. The brief treatment in this chapter depends heavily on the more extensive analysis and documentation especially in Richard Horsley, *Jesus and the Spiral of Violence: Popular Jewish Resistance in Roman Palestine* (San Francisco: Harper & Row, 1987), chapters 1-4; *Sociology and the Jesus Movement* (New York: Crossroad, 1989), chapters 4 and 5; *Galilee: History, Politics, People* (Valley Forge: Trinity, 1995); *Scribes, Visionaries, and the Politics of Second Temple Judea* (Louisville: Westminster John Knox, 2007), chapters 4-6; Anthony J. Saldarini, *Pharisees, Scribes, and Sadducees in Palestinian Society* (Wilmington: Glazier, 1988), chapters 2-4. Saldarini and others have applied the comparative historical sociology of Gerhard Lenski, especially *Power and Privilege: A Theory of Social Stratification* (New York: McGraw, 1966), to advantage, particularly in discerning the role of the scribes and Pharisees as "retainers" of the Jerusalem temple-state. While more helpful than other structural-functional sociological models, which were largely abandoned by sociologists after the 1960s, Lenski's analysis in terms of social

The fundamental social form in Roman Palestine, as in any traditional agrarian society, was the village community, comprised of many multigenerational families or households. The vast majority of the population lived in hundreds of larger or smaller villages, surrounded by the fields that the families farmed (Josephus, *The Jewish War* 3.41-47). Josephus mentions that there were 204 such villages in Galilee, a number consistent with modern archaeological surveys (*Life* 235). Each village was a semi-self-governing community. Local affairs were conducted in a local assembly (called a *synagōgē* or *knesset* in the Gospels and rabbinic texts respectively) led by local "elders."[4]

The constituent families of the villages were also the fundamental unit of production. Families produced nearly all the food they consumed and consumed much of what they produced — what was left after payment of tithes, taxes, tribute, and interest on loans. As the fundamental units of production, village families were also the economic base from which the rulers derived their revenues, in the forms of tribute, taxes, tithes and offerings. According to the Judean historian Josephus, the Romans knew, presumably on the basis of their census, just how much could be taken from the villagers (*Jewish Antiquities* 14.202-3; 17.318-20). Many families lived at the subsistence level. Dearth and hunger were common.

As indicated by the term "Roman Palestine," the overall ruler was Rome. Completing the Roman takeover of the eastern Mediterranean lands and peoples, the warlord Pompey had conquered Palestine in 63 BCE. The Romans laid the people under tribute, which was meant as a humiliation as well as a source of imperial revenue, fixing the rate at 25% of the crop every second year (except sabbatical years, when the land was supposedly left fallow; see *Antiquities* 14.202-3). For the next several generations in Palestine, as elsewhere in the southeastern Mediterranean lands, the Romans ruled through local client kings and other rulers, who became the face of Roman power. Initially, Rome kept intact the temple-state in Jerusalem headed by the Hasmonean high priest Hyr-

---

stratification tends to obscure the power-relations in the fundamental division between rulers and ruled in traditional agrarian societies. See the critique in Horsley, *Scribes, Visionaries,* chapter 3.

4. See Horsley, *Galilee,* chapter 10.

canus II. In order to establish tighter control after recurrent uprisings led by rivals to the Hasmonean high priesthood, the Roman Senate appointed the military strongman Herod "king of the Judeans" in 40 BCE. After conquering his subjects with the aid of Roman troops, Herod ruled and taxed all the districts of Palestine from 37 to 4 BCE. He retained the Jerusalem temple as an instrument of his own rule and appointed high priests in service of his own political purposes.

After Herod's death, the Romans divided his territory and placed different client rulers over different districts (*Antiquities* 17.317-20). They appointed Herod's son Antipas as "tetrarch" over Galilee and Perea (east of the Jordan). For the first time in the history of the region, the ruler of Galilee established his residence and administration in the district, in two cities he built there, Sepphoris and Tiberias. Over the area northeast of Galilee Rome appointed Philip, another son of Herod, who built up the town of Bethsaida by the lake as one of his capitals. Over Judea and Samaria Caesar initially placed Herod's son Archelaus. After ten years of turmoil, however, the Romans deposed Archelaus and ruled the people through the Judean priesthood that Herod had left intact, now under the close supervision of a Roman governor vested with the power to appoint and depose high priests. During the lifetime of Jesus, then, Galilee and Judea were under different rulers.

Ever since it had been established under the Persian Empire, the temple-state in Jerusalem had served as a local instrument of imperial control and taxation. Under Herod and then especially under direct Roman supervision, the high priesthood became all the more dependent on, and submissive to, imperial rule. Successive governors appointed new high priests with some frequency (*Antiquities* 20.224-51), always from the four high priestly families Herod had brought into the priestly aristocracy. The temple and high priesthood continued as the center of the economy in Judea, the temple serving, in effect, as a bank as well as the place for sacrifices and pilgrimage festivals, which of course contributed to the economic centralization of Jerusalem. The high priestly aristocracy was also charged with collection of the tribute to Rome. The priestly aristocracy at the head of the temple-state in Jerusalem thus became, effectively, the face of Roman imperial rule in Judea (the subject of much of *War* 2).

While there was no middle class in ancient Judea, there were people "in the middle" between the rulers and the villagers, yet all more or less dependent on the rulers. The Jerusalem scribe Ben Sira mentions, for example, artisans of various kinds who served the needs of the temple and the desires of the wealthy aristocracy (Sir 38:27-32). Far more important for the operation of the temple-state in Jerusalem, however, were the "scribes," who served as advisors to the ruling priestly aristocracy and who cultivated Judean traditions and religious norms (38:33–39:4).[5] The importance of the scribes is attested, ironically, in the modern (mis)understanding of Josephus's descriptions of the "philosophies" or "parties" *(haireseis)* of the Judeans — Pharisees, Sadducees, Essenes — as "sects" within "Judaism." The Sadducees have long been thought to be roughly the same as the wealthy priestly aristocrats. The Essenes are now thought to be the same as or at least similar to the priests and scribes who had withdrawn from the temple-state in protest to form the Qumran community in the wilderness of Judea.

The Pharisees, to whom Josephus repeatedly attributes the most "accurate" knowledge of the ancestral laws, were evidently the dominant "party" of the scribes. From his accounts it seems clear that the Pharisees functioned as what historical sociologists call the intellectual-legal "retainers" of the Judean temple-state (*Antiquities* 13.288-98; 14.408-10). Contrary to a view that became prominent about a generation ago, the Pharisees did not drop out of Judean politics and withdraw to pious eating clubs under the tyranny of Herod the Great.[6] Josephus is clear that they served at Herod's court, albeit with greatly reduced influence (*Antiquities* 17.41, 44, 46). The most important indication of their continuing role in the governing of Judea in the first century is Josephus's indication that "leading Pharisees" played a prominent role in the provisional government headed by high priests who remained in Jerusalem in an attempt to control the popular revolt in 66-70 CE (*Life* 21, 197-99).

---

5. Fuller analysis and documentation in Horsley, *Scribes, Visionaries,* chapters 3-5.

6. Compare, e.g., Jacob Neusner, *From Politics to Piety* (Englewood Cliffs: Prentice-Hall, 1973), with more recent critical analyses such as Steve Mason, *Flavius Josephus on the Pharisees: A Composition-Critical Study* (Leiden: Brill, 1991).

The Dynamics of Imperial Rule

When the people of Galilee and Judea resisted and sometimes rebelled against Roman rule, the Roman reconquests were more violent and destructive than the initial conquest. The Romans even viewed failure to pay the tribute in timely fashion as tantamount to rebellion and reacted with gruesome vengeance. In recent decades, historians of the Roman Empire have become much more candid about the brutality of Roman imperial tactics.[7] Standard Roman practice was to terrorize the peoples they conquered by destroying villages, slaughtering or enslaving the people, and crucifying resistance leaders along the public ways. In words placed in the mouth of a Caledonian chieftain by the Roman historian Tacitus, "[The Romans are] the plunderers of the world. . . . If the enemy is rich, they are rapacious; if poor, they lust for dominion. Not East, not West has sated them. . . . They rob, butcher, plunder and call it 'empire'; they make a desolation and call it 'peace'" (*Agricola* 29-38).[8]

Josephus offers many similar descriptions of the Roman conquest and reconquests of areas of Palestine, ranging from Pompey's original incursion in 63 BCE to the devastation of the countryside and destruction of Jerusalem and the temple in 67-70 CE. When towns and villages were slow to pay an extraordinary levy of tribute imposed on Syria and Palestine, the warlord Cassius sold village elders as slaves and enslaved the people of four district towns in Judea, including Emmaus (*Antiquities* 14.271-75). The Roman reconquest of Galilee and Judea to put down the revolt after Herod's death in 4 BCE wrought extensive destruction and terrorization of the people (*War* 2.66-75; *Antiquities* 17.288-95). Led by Varus, Roman legions advancing through Galilee burned the town of Sepphoris, near Nazareth, and enslaved its people. In Judea, Varus ordered the town of Emmaus destroyed, then scoured the countryside for leaders of the insurrection and had two thousand crucified. The brutal Roman reconquest thus left long-lasting collective trauma in its wake just at the time Jesus was born.

---

7. See, e.g., Susan P. Mattern, *Rome and the Enemy: Imperial Strategy in the Principate* (Berkeley: University of California, 1999); J. E. Lendon, *Empire of Honor* (Oxford: Oxford University Press, 1997).

8. Adapted by the authors from the Loeb edition, trans. M. Hutton and R. Ogilvie (Cambridge: Harvard University Press, 1980).

The effects of Roman rule were also economic. It took Herod the Great three years to conquer his subjects with the aid of Rome-supplied troops, particularly against the persistently resistant Galileans. Thereafter Herod's impact on the people was primarily economic. He was as ambitious as he was tyrannical. His expenses were monumental, the produce of the peasantry being his principal economic base. Herod established a luxurious court in Jerusalem, lavished gifts on the emperor Augustus and his family, funded numerous public works in cities throughout the empire, and even set up an endowment for the funding of the Olympic games (*War* 1.422-28).

Most remarkable were Herod's massive building projects in his own realm. He established garrisoned fortresses around the countryside for security, of which Masada was only the most famous. He built two completely new cities named in honor of Augustus, the seaport Caesarea on the coast and Sebaste (Greek for "Augustus") on the site of the previously destroyed Samaria, along with several temples in honor of Caesar. He built Roman institutions such as a hippodrome and amphitheater in Jerusalem. Perhaps his most ambitious project was the rebuilding not just of the Jerusalem temple but of the whole temple mount. "Herod's temple," which was not completed until just before the great revolt of 66-73, became one of the wonders of the Roman world. Fitting its grand Hellenistic-Roman style was its imperial decor, particularly the golden eagle over one of the gates, symbolizing the subordination of the temple to the empire with its regular sacrifices in honor of Roma and Caesar (*Antiquities* 17.151). All this massive construction was supported by taxation of the people. Protest of the excessive tax-burden was futile, although Herod was wise enough to know when to ease up (as in times of drought and famine) lest he destroy the economic base on which he was dependent.

After the death of Herod, the Romans placed his sons in power over the different regions of his realm. In Galilee and Perea, Antipas, who had been raised at the imperial court in Rome, continued in his footsteps. He built his first capital city on the site of the town of Sepphoris, near the village of Nazareth (*Antiquities* 18.27). Within twenty years, however, he built a second capital city named for the emperor Tiberius overlooking the Sea of Galilee, complete with an elaborate royal palace. According to Josephus's account, the building of Tiberias involved the destruction of villages and displacement of many villagers, some of whom were evidently forced to become laborers in the new city (*Antiquities* 18.36-38). With rule of Galilee established in the region itself for the first time in history, Antipas could gather revenues more efficiently from these capital cities, which commanded views over nearly every village in lower Galilee.

Herod's son Philip, appointed by the Romans over the district to the northeast of Galilee, rebuilt the large village of Bethsaida as one of his capitals and built Caesarea Philippi further north as another, with another imperial temple nearby (*Antiquities* 18.28). The expansion of Bethsaida, just east across the Jordan river from Capernaum, would have involved a population displacement similar to what had occurred in and around Tiberias, all in the first two decades of Jesus' lifetime.

Ten years after Herod's death, the Romans deposed his son Archelaus and placed Judea under the control of the high priestly aristocracy, the four families that Herod had elevated to positions of power and privilege, who operated by appointment and oversight of Roman governors based in Caesarea, Herod's Mediterranean port city. The Jerusalem high priesthood had no choice but to collaborate closely in Roman rule of Judea. The priestly aristocracy has often been referred to as "Jewish leaders." But Josephus's accounts of conflicts between Judeans and Roman rule mention no case in which they provided leadership for the people in representing their interests to the Romans.[9] Rather they stood with the Romans, who held them accountable to maintain order as well as to gather tribute.

Indeed, the four families from which the Roman governor made appointments to the office of high priest evidently used their position of power and privilege to expand their own wealth. As suggested by archaeological exploration in Jerusalem, they evidently constructed ever more elaborate mansions for themselves in the course of the first century. Josephus provides one revealing window onto their blatantly predatory behavior vis-à-vis Judean villagers, with adverse effects on the ordinary

9. For further analysis, documentation, and discussion, see Richard Horsley, "The High Priests and the Politics of Roman Palestine," *Journal for the Study of Judaism* 17 (1986), 23-55; and Martin Goodman, *The Ruling Class of Judaea* (Cambridge: Cambridge University Press, 1987).

priests as well: the high priest Ananias sent his hired thugs to the village threshing floors to take by force the tithes meant for the regular priests, beating those who refused to yield their produce. Other high priests followed suit, the people powerless to stop them (*Antiquities* 20.181, 206-7). The predatory and repressive practices of the high priests became legendary, as indicated by the following memory in the Talmud (*bPesahim* 57a) generations later:

> Woe to me because of the house of Baithos;
> Woe to me because of their lances!
> Woe to me because of the house of Hanan (Ananus). . . .
> Woe to me because of the house of Kathros. . . .
> Woe to me because of the house of Ishmael ben Phiabi,
> Woe to me because of their fists.
> For they are high priests
> and their sons are treasurers
> and their sons-in-law are temple overseers
> and their servants smite the people with staves!

It is not difficult to imagine the effect on the people of multiple layers of rulers and their demands for revenues. Those left without enough food to survive after the officers of their rulers had taken tithes, taxes, and tribute from the top of the piles of grain on the threshing floors were forced to borrow (perhaps often from those same officers) at high rates of interest. Many families fell into spiraling debt and, if they did not lose control of their ancestral land, became subservient to their creditors. The high priests and Herodians in Judea and the Herodian officers in Galilee were only too willing to make loans, at high rates of interest.[10] This was the traditional mechanism by which the wealthy and powerful could bring villagers under their control to exact further revenues and even take control over their land. There is evidence that Herodian and high priestly families did just this in northwestern Judea by the middle of

10. See Martin Goodman, "The First Jewish Revolt: Social Conflict and the Problem of Debt," in Geza Vermes and Jacob Neusner, eds., *Essays in Honor of Yigael Yadin* (Oxford: Oxford Center for Postgraduate Hebrew Studies, 1982); Magen Broshi, "The Role of the Temple in the Herodian Economy," *Journal of Jewish Studies* 38 (1987), 31-38.

the first century CE, reducing peasants to tenants on their former ancestral lands.[11]

Popular Revolts, Protests, and Resistance Movements

The people of Roman Palestine did not simply acquiesce in their subjugation and exploitation. Villagers usually submit, however unwillingly, to their circumstances — rather than suffer harsh treatment and death or enslavement. They are adept at hidden forms of resistance.[12] But rarely do peasants mount revolts or even sustained movements of resistance. The Palestinian villagers rooted in Israelite traditions of resistance, however, were unusual in antiquity. More than any other subject people in the Roman Empire, Judeans and Galileans resisted imperial rule and periodically revolted against their rulers.

The mission of Jesus was framed by two widespread revolts against the Romans and their client rulers in Jerusalem and Galilee. After the death of the demanding and repressive Herod the Great, revolt erupted in most major districts of his realm, Judea, Galilee, and Perea (*War* 2.56-65; *Antiquities* 17.271-84). The people of Jerusalem clamored for a new high priest who would serve more in accord with justice and the law. Villagers in Galilee and Judea successfully asserted their independence for a year or more, before Varus and his legions brutally suppressed the revolt. Just over thirty years after Jesus' mission, in 66 CE, the people again mounted a widespread revolt in Galilee as well as Judea, the subject of Josephus's *Jewish War* (see especially the last sections of *War* 2). The people of Jerusalem expelled the Romans from the city, and peasant forces from the countryside drove them out of Judea. The high priestly aristocrats took refuge in the temple and the Rome-appointed rulers in Galilee took refuge in their fortified cities. The people's independence lasted only a year in Galilee before Roman troops again wrought devastation,

11. David Fiensy, *The Social History of Palestine in the Herodian Period* (Lewiston: Mellen, 1991), 32-43.

12. See especially James C. Scott, *Weapons of the Weak: Everyday Forms of Peasant Resistance* (New Haven: Yale University Press, 1985), and *Domination and the Arts of Resistance: Hidden Transcripts* (New Haven: Yale University Press, 1990).

slaughter, and enslavement. In Judea, the uneasy independence lasted nearly four years before the Romans destroyed Jerusalem and the temple after devastating the countryside.

The great "Jewish revolt" of 66-73 is often understood as a struggle of "the Jews" in general against the Romans. Ironically, our primary historical source for this conflict, the Judean historian Josephus, has invited this uncritical view by portraying some of the high priests and "leading Pharisees" as a kind of a provisional junta in Jerusalem and himself as the heroic enemy general leading the Jewish forces against the great Roman general Vespasian, who ascended to the imperial throne in the middle of the conflict (69 CE). But Josephus also indicates clearly that the high priests and other elites, including himself, only feigned preparation for war while attempting to control the volatile situation until they could negotiate with the Romans (*War* 2.562-68, 651-54; 4.319-22; and generally his *Life*).[13]

Josephus also provides vivid accounts of the vehement hostility of the ordinary Jerusalemites and villagers toward their high priestly and Herodian rulers. The people evidently were fully aware of the source of their economic exploitation. Soon after the conflict began, they burned the archives in Jerusalem to destroy the records of debts (*War* 2.427) and sacked the mansion of the high priest Ananias, one of the most predatory as well as powerful (former) high priests (2.428-29). Popular bands attacked other high priestly figures and Herodians, almost certainly individuals who had maneuvered them into debt and taken control of their ancestral lands. The four major fighting groups that maintained the people's independence for several years and finally retreated into Jerusalem and the fortified temple to withstand the Roman forces of reconquest were all from the countryside (all evident from Josephus's accounts in *War* 3 and 4). These revolts were the most dramatic overt expression of the continuing dynamic conflict inherent in the political-economic-religious structure of Roman Palestine.

Between the widespread and outright revolts of 4 BCE and 66 CE, resistance persisted in a series of popular protests and movements and even organized protests by dissident scribal groups. It is clear from

---

13. See further Horsley, *Galilee*, 72-75.

Josephus's accounts that all these protests and movements were rooted in Israelite tradition and Mosaic covenantal principles. We focus here on several that also illustrate both significant features of the popular or scribal ability to organize collective action and the structural conflict in which villagers and some scribal retainers stood with their rulers, both Roman and Roman clients.

In 40 CE, the plan of the emperor Gaius (Caligula) to install a bust of himself in the Jerusalem temple by force of arms evoked a widespread and well-organized peasant "strike" (*Antiquities* 18.261-74; Philo, *Legatio ad Gaium* 225-26). Knowing that the tribute taken by Caesar depended on their crops the next fall, Galilean villagers refused to plant their fields as the Roman troops advanced through their district in the spring. This response is often explained as motivated only by the commandment against images. These Galilean peasants, however, appear to have been motivated by a combination of the first and second commandments, which deal with more than mere "images": the prohibition of having any other gods other than God (Gaius was retaliating against Jews who refused to honor him as divine) and the prohibition of bowing down and yielding tribute to the gods represented by those "images."[14]

Most significant, surely, for comparison with Jesus' mission and the movement(s) he catalyzed were the two types of popular movements of resistance and renewal that took distinctively Israelite forms. One was the social form taken by the revolts in 4 BCE and the largest of the resistance movements in the great revolt of 66-70.[15] In these popular *messianic* movements, Judean and Galilean rebels acclaimed their leaders "kings." Movements of this kind were patterned after the formative event of the anointing of the bandit chieftain David (2 Sam 2:1-4; 5:1-4) to lead the resistance against the Philistines. Led by marginal figures such as the shepherd Athronges in Judea and Judas son of the bandit chieftain Hezekiah in Galilee, these movements attacked Roman baggage trains or local royal fortresses to "take back" some of the goods that had been seized and stored there. These groups maintained the people's independence

14. Further analysis and discussion in Horsley, *Jesus and the Spiral,* 110-16.

15. Analysis and discussion of texts and movements in Richard Horsley, "Popular Messianic Movements Around the Time of Jesus," *Catholic Biblical Quarterly* 46 (1984), 471-93.

(eleutheria) of Herodian or high priestly rule for a year or more after Herod's death before the Romans could subjugate them again.

The other type, the popular *prophetic* movements that emerged in mid-first-century CE Judea and Samaria, patterned themselves after acts of deliverance that were formative for Israel as a people: the exodus led by Moses and/or the struggles against Canaanite kings led by Joshua. Of the many such movements, three are best known. In 36 CE, a Samaritan prophet led a large band of followers to Mount Gerizim — in Samaritan lore, the site where Joshua and the tribes had built an altar and renewed the covenant after entering the promised land — where he promised to unearth sacred vessels left there by Moses (*Antiquities* 18.85-87). Ten years later in Judea, the prophet Theudas led his followers to the Jordan River, promising that the waters would divide so they could pass through (*Antiquities* 20.97-99). In a third example from the late 50s CE, famous for its mention in Acts 21:38, a (Judean) prophet who had come (returned) from Egypt led his followers to the Mount of Olives (the predicted site of God's advent to restore his people in Zechariah 14) and claimed that the walls of the city would fall, just as the walls of Jericho had fallen before Joshua (*War* 2.261-63; *Antiquities* 20.167-72). These prophets and their people were caught up in anticipation of new divine acts of deliverance that would result in the restoration of the people's freedom from rulers in their land.[16] Sensing the danger of revolt, the Romans sent out the military, killed the prophets and their followers, and dispersed the movements.

Even some of the scribal retainers whose role was to serve the temple-state took action in resistance to the Romans and/or the Roman

---

16. See further Richard Horsley, "Popular Prophetic Movements at the Time of Jesus, Their Principal Features and Social Origins," *Journal for the Study of the New Testament* 26 (1986), 3-27. These prophets have been labeled "sign prophets," perhaps under the influence of the "signs" performed by Jesus in John's Gospel. Josephus does use the terms "signs" and "tokens" in his summary passages, but not in his accounts of particular prophets and their movements. He seems to mean that they acted in imitation of Moses and/or Joshua in the exodus and entry into the land, a standard use of such terms. The label "sign-prophets" however, is misleading in at least two senses: the prophets were not performing or anticipating signs of some other deliverance, but deliverance itself, as with the foundational events they were patterned after; and the "signs and tokens" in Josephus's summaries are not comparable to the "signs" Jesus does in John's Gospel.

client rulers on whom they were dependent.[17] In a brazen act of defiance against Rome, Herod, and the temple just before the king's death, two of the most highly regarded Jerusalem sages inspired their students to cut down the golden Roman eagle from above the temple gate (*War* 1.648-55; *Antiquities* 17.149-67). In a brutal act of intimidation, Herod ordered the sages and their students burned alive at a public assembly.

Some ten years later, as the Romans were setting the high priesthood in charge of Judea under direct supervision of a Roman governor, the leaders of what Josephus calls the "Fourth Philosophy," comprised of dissident scribal teachers such as Judas of Gamala and radical Pharisees such as Saddok, organized resistance to the tribute (*Antiquities* 18.4-5, 23). They insisted that payment of the tribute was a violation of the first two covenantal commandments, compromising Israel's exclusive loyalty to its sole divine ruler and master.

Decades later, in the turbulent years leading up to the great revolt, as the high priestly figures continued to collaborate in repressive Roman rule and became ever more predatory on their own people, dissident scribes even resorted to terrorist acts. Their actions were clearly protests against Roman rule, but targeted native figures who headed the Judean temple-state. In the anonymity and protection of milling crowds at festivals in the temple courtyard, the *Sicarii* or "dagger men" (a name derived from the curved daggers they hid in their clothing) assassinated a number of prominent citizens, including even a high priest (*War* 2.254-57). As we know from studies of modern terrorism, it is when subject peoples feel that less violent channels of protest are denied to them that they resort to such desperate acts — in this historical context, in response to Rome's ongoing terrorization of the people in military actions and periodic crucifixions of suspected rebels.

That responses of this kind were generated not only by ordinary people but also by dissident scribal and Pharisaic retainers reveals that even

---

17. For further discussion of these actions of scribal resistance, see Richard Horsley, *Revolt of the Scribes: Resistance and Apocalyptic Origins* (Minneapolis: Fortress, 2010), chapter 10. These scribal protests were distinctively different from the Zealots proper, who originated as a coalition of popular groups in the middle of the revolt of 66-70, as explained in Richard Horsley, "The Zealots, Their Origin, Relationships, and Importance in the Jewish Revolt," *Novum Testamentum* 28 (1986), 159-92.

those who served and represented the Jerusalem temple-state were opposed to, and ready to take action against, the high priestly rulers and their Roman patrons.

The Cultural Divide

It is ironic that interpreters of Jesus and the Gospels, who focus almost exclusively on religion in isolation from politics and economics, have tended to neglect a key component of the cultural divide in ancient Palestine, one that corresponded to the basic political-economic division between the villagers and the rulers with their retainers. In this connection even more than in connection with the political-economic structure and dynamics, the standard concept of "Judaism" has tended to block recognition. Apparently assuming that most people in antiquity could read and that Jesus' contemporaries had ready access to sacred documents, Scripture scholars have taken extant Judean texts such as Daniel, Sirach, the *Psalms of Solomon,* and *Jubilees* as evidence of the beliefs of "Jews" in general.

Extensive recent research, however, has shown that literacy in antiquity was severely limited, confined basically to an educated elite (see chapter 4 below).[18] In Judea the literate elite were the scribes and Pharisees, the legal-intellectual retainers who served the temple-state. The extant written texts from late second temple times represent the views of the literate elite, not the attitudes of the people generally. Recent research has also shown that written scrolls were costly and cumbersome, confined basically to the temple and scribal circles, such as the community at Qumran. Extensive excavations by archaeologists to find ancient synagogue buildings, moreover, have found virtually no first-century buildings that might have had "Torah shrines" housing scrolls of Scriptures — which villagers could not have read in the first place.[19] Thus,

18. William V. Harris, *Ancient Literacy* (Cambridge, MA: Harvard University Press, 1989); Catherine Hezser, *Jewish Literacy in Roman Palestine* (Tübingen: Mohr Siebeck, 2001).

19. While archaeologists have claimed to find earlier synagogue buildings at the Herodian fortresses of Masada and Herodium, in Gamla east of the Sea of Galilee, and Magdala, they date most of the buildings that seem more clearly to have been places of

while ordinary people knew of the existence of the scrolls and may have known some of the content that stood "written" in "the Law and the Prophets," they probably did not have much direct contact with those written documents. And there is no clear evidence that the Jerusalem scribes and Pharisees traveled from village to village "reading" to the people from cumbersome scrolls.

Despite having little direct knowledge of written scrolls of "the Law and Prophets," however, the people were by no means ignorant of Israelite tradition. Like other traditional peasantries, they cultivated orally what anthropologists call their own "little traditions," which paralleled the "great tradition" that was cultivated in writing as well as orally by the (literate) cultural elite.[20] As in similar societies, there would have been considerable overlap between the popular and the official traditions, so that the two shared foundational stories (the exodus, David's reign, Elijah and Elisha), customs (circumcision, Sabbath), and celebrations (Passover). The covenantal commandments and many covenantal teachings and mechanisms, such as the sabbatical year fallow of the land and the seventh year release of debts, would have been cultivated and, evidently, practiced in the conduct of social-economic life in village communities, the sacred laws and regulations known from traditional teachings and lifeways rather than from scrolls of Deuteronomy. However, insofar as Israelite popular tradition carried and expressed the interests and concerns of the villagers, it would have had different emphases from the official tradition cultivated by the scribal circles in Jerusalem, which articulated the interests of the temple-state.

Since non-literate peasants do not usually leave written records, evidence for popular tradition emerges mainly when the people take action, as in the popular messianic and prophetic movements mentioned just above. The patterns of these movements indicate that collective memo-

---

assembly in Galilean villages to late antiquity. See the summary of the evidence and discussion, with references, in Richard Horsley, *Archaeology, History, and Society in Galilee: The Social Context of Jesus and the Rabbis* (Harrisburg: Trinity, 1996), 132-45.

20. See especially James C. Scott, "Protest and Profanation: Agrarian Revolt and the Little Tradition," *Theory and Society* 4 (1977), 1-38, 211-46; application to the Gospels (and Jesus) in Richard Horsley, *Jesus in Context: Power, People, and Performance* (Minneapolis: Fortress, 2008), 68-71, 151-56, 207-10.

ries of the young David leading the Israelites against the Philistines and
of Moses and Joshua leading the Israelites through the exodus and into
their land were prominent among the villagers.[21] The popular Israelite
tradition cultivated by villagers at the time of Jesus thus included the social memory of two distinct forms of leaders and movements, and this
widespread popular memory provided established cultural patterns for
new leaders and movements that sought the renewal of Israel on its land
in independence of invasive and oppressive rulers. There are a number of
other indications of the Israelite cultural tradition cultivated among the
people. For example, Josephus mentions several incidents of Galileans'
objections to acts that he or other more aristocratic agents took during
the great revolt in 66-67 CE. Their objections were rooted in the principles of the Mosaic covenant, which would presumably have been well
known among people of Israelite heritage.[22]

Perhaps the most dramatic illustration of the differences between
popular tradition and official scribal tradition may be taken from the an-
nual celebration of Passover. Villagers did not need to be literate to know
the story of the people's deliverance from bondage under Pharaoh in
Egypt: they recited and celebrated that story every year at Passover. Centuries before Jesus, however, Passover had become a week-long festival
celebrated in Jerusalem, as part of the political-economic-religious centralization of Judean life in the temple. Because of the frequent excitement of the people at the celebration of their formative deliverance and
independence of foreign rule, the Roman governors established the regular practice of bringing troops into the city and posting them atop the
colonnade of the temple courtyard to keep order (*War* 2.223-25; *Antiquities* 20.106-8). But this only exacerbated the ironic juxtaposition of the
people's celebration of their ancient liberation from Egypt with their current subjugation to Rome. At a Passover celebration in the late 40s CE, a
Roman soldier stationed atop the temple porticoes made a lewd gesture
to the Passover crowd, leading the mob to pelt the soldiers with stones;

21. For the introduction of the important concept of "social memory" into New
Testament studies, see Alan Kirk and Tom Thatcher, eds., *Memory, Tradition, and Text:
Uses of the Past in Early Christianity* (Semeia Studies 52; Atlanta: Society of Biblical Liter-
ature, 2004).

22. Analysis of Josephus's accounts is in Horsley, *Galilee*, 152-55.

the governor, Cumanus, responded by sending more soldiers to disperse the crowd, ultimately causing a deadly stampede in the courtyard. Because of the different emphases and outright contradictory implications in the popular and the official traditions and their observance, the Passover festival was a highly-charged occasion of acute tension and potential overt conflict.

For the official tradition of the Jerusalem rulers and retainers we have considerable written evidence, including the multiple versions of the Scriptures that were later included in the Hebrew Bible. Books of Mosaic Torah had been composed to lend authority to the temple-state. From the Dead Sea Scrolls, however, we now know that books of alternative Torah, such as the Temple Scroll and the book of *Jubilees,* also had authority in certain scribal circles. The writing of key texts on large scrolls gave them added authority as Scripture. Because the learned scribes had these key texts written on the tablets of their heart, however, we should not imagine that they regularly consulted written scrolls (see further in chapter 4). The cultivation of "Mosaic" Torah, moreover, was not confined to the books that were later included in the Hebrew Bible. The Sadducees, according to Josephus, held that only those books of Moses that were "written" held authority. The Pharisees, however, promulgated and cultivated additional Mosaic Torah in their "traditions of the elders." Josephus includes a fascinating incident at the opening of the great revolt in 66 CE that is most suggestive for the ad hoc operation even of the official tradition (*War* 2.409-17). The temple captain Eleazar and other priests at one point refused to continue to make offerings (from strangers) in honor of Caesar. The (other) high priests objected and brought in experts in the laws of the Judeans to attest the legality of the offerings. But evidently neither side appealed to a written text of Torah.

Given the mediating social position and role of the scribal retainers, cultivation of the official tradition did not operate solely in support and legitimation of the temple and its high priestly aristocracy. As noted above, scribal retainers, as advisers in the administration of the temple-state and cultivators of the Israelite "great tradition," were often caught between their high-priestly superiors, who were beholden to the Romans, and their loyalty to Israelite tradition, recorded in and symbolized by the sacred writings. The official Judean tradition had incorporated Israelite traditions such as the exodus, the Mosaic covenant, and many teachings that expressed the interests and ostensibly protected the rights of the people. It had also incorporated prophetic oracles and exhortations against earlier rulers. Scribes were repeatedly placed in an awkward position when the high priestly rulers collaborated closely with the imperial rulers, often in violation of covenant law as well as ideals in other Israelite traditions, such as the exodus liberation.

Some scribal circles reacted or protested. Both the scribal teachers who inspired their students to cut the Roman eagle down from atop the temple gate and the scribal teacher and Pharisee who led the resistance to the Roman tribute were acting in defense of the first two commandments of the Mosaic covenant. Most remarkable was the large group of scribes and priests who withdrew into the wilderness at Qumran in protest against the incumbent high priesthood, as attested in their distinctive texts found among the Dead Sea Scrolls. As indicated in their Community Rule and Damascus Rule, they identified with the exodus-covenant core of Israelite tradition, making a new exodus into the wilderness and establishing a renewal of Israelite covenant community.

It is thus clear from recent research that there was a fundamental cultural divide that corresponded to the political-economic division between the villagers who cultivated their own popular tradition orally and "the scribes and Pharisees" who served the temple-state. Yet the Israelite popular tradition cultivated in village communities and the "great tradition" cultivated by scribal circles in Jerusalem were similar in their core, so that some scribal views and actions paralleled popular movements of resistance.

CHAPTER TWO

Regional Histories, Shared Tradition, and the Renewal of Israel

———— ∞ ————

The Israelite people demonstrated remarkable resilience through a series of disruptive historical events over many centuries. The people of the different regions of Palestine experienced dramatically different histories, yet continued to share a formative cultural tradition, despite the different forms and emphases this tradition took among the common people in the various regions and in the scribal circles in Jerusalem. As we probe ever more sensitively into late second temple Judean sources, it is striking how widespread and strong was the drive not just to resist the Romans and their client rulers in Jerusalem, but to effect a renewal of the people on their land. The longing for renewal, sometimes fueling overt resistance, was particularly strong among the people but also manifest in scribal circles.

The continuing projection of the broad construct "Judaism/the Jews" onto the people of Palestine under Roman rule obscures important evidence from the sources regarding regional differences, the variety among the many movements of renewal, and the fundamental religious-political-economic divide between the rulers and the ruled. A review of the different but related histories of the people in the various regions of Israelite heritage and a critical survey of late second temple Judean texts may provide a more appropriate sense of the historical context of the portrayals of Jesus' mission in the Gospels generally and the Gospel of John particularly.

Shared Israelite Tradition, Different Regional Histories

According to common Israelite tradition, Israel originated as an independent people in the exodus from bondage in Egypt led by the prototypical prophet Moses. The tribes of Israel claimed common ancestors in Abraham and the other patriarchs and matriarchs. In their early history, they lived in tribal clans in the hill country of Palestine, each independent but all guided by a common allegiance to the principles of the Mosaic covenant under the direct rule (kingship) of God. In the early (northern Israelite) "Song of Deborah" (Judges 5) it is assumed that all the tribes should come to the aid of those under attack by outside rulers, but only those in the immediate area, in that case the hills of Galilee, evidently responded to the call. In order to maintain their independence of the Philistines, the Israelites came together more significantly as they "anointed" the young warrior David as military leader in a conditional, popular kingship. When David and then his son Solomon set up a more imperial monarchy, however, the Israelites rebelled (2 Samuel 15–18, 20; 1 Kings 12).

Different Regional Histories

According to the Deuteronomistic history, only the tribe of Judah, along with the smaller tribe of Benjamin and at least some Levites, remained under the Davidic dynasty in Jerusalem after Solomon. The tiny kingdom of Judah managed to maintain its semi-independence even under the oversight of successive foreign empires. The ten northern tribes, however, set up a more conditional kingship. When Ahab consolidated the power of the monarchy in violation of Mosaic covenantal principles, the prophets Elijah and his protégé Elisha led popular resistance. According to popular traditions that were taken into the official Judean tradition (1 Kings 17–2 Kings 9), Elijah and Elisha were associated with a larger band of inspired prophets, with whose help Elijah attempted to rally a renewal of all the Israelite people, symbolized by the altar of "twelve stones" in the famous contest between Elijah and the prophets of Baal. Elijah was also commissioned to "anoint" a popular figure to lead the people against king Ahab, which Elisha eventually carried out, and both Elijah and Elisha performed wondrous acts of healing and multiplication of food for needy people. The monarchy in northern Israel survived this prophetic challenge, but a century later was conquered by the Assyrian Empire, in two stages (2 Kgs 15:29-31; 17:1-6). The Assyrians placed the villagers of Galilee under the direct rule of imperial administrators based in the fortified town of Megiddo, while villagers of the central hill country were placed under client kings (and later an aristocracy) in Samaria.

In 587 BCE, Babylonian armies destroyed Jerusalem and Solomon's temple and deported the ruling families of Judah to Babylon, leaving surviving villagers on the land (2 Kings 24–25). The Persian Empire, taking over from the Babylonians, sent some of the deported Judean families back to the ruins of Jerusalem to rebuild the temple of their ancestral God.[1] But this return of the Judean elite from "the exile" can hardly be understood as the beginnings of an independent "Judaism." Rather, the emerging priestly aristocracy of the tiny Jerusalem temple-state, sponsored and funded by the Persians, served as the local representatives of the imperial administration, responsible for maintaining order and rendering tribute to the imperial court.

Evidently, the Persian imperial regime also sponsored or encouraged the consolidation of local Judean laws and customs.[2] During the first several centuries of the "second temple" period, circles of Judean scribes and priests gathered Judean-Israelite historical traditions, legal collections, and prophetic oracles into composite texts. Consolidated and composed as books with the added aura of having been "written" on scrolls, these texts, laid up in the new temple, provided added "authority" to the temple-state.[3] Many of these Scriptures, later included in what we now know as "the Hebrew Bible," reflect an insistence that the Samar-

---

1. Some of the extensive recent critical analysis and discussion of the sparsely attested history of early second temple Judea is summarized in Richard Horsley, *Scribes, Visionaries, and the Politics of Second Temple Judea* (Louisville: Westminster John Knox, 2007), chapters 1 and 2.

2. See James W. Watts, ed., *Persia and Torah* (Atlanta: Society of Biblical Literature, 2001), especially the essays by Joseph Blenkinsopp and Lisbet Fried.

3. For discussion on the basis of recent research, see Horsley, *Scribes, Visionaries,* chapter 6.

itans, along with "the peoples of the land," were ethnically and religiously impure (2 Kings 17; Ezra 4:1-5; 9–10; Nehemiah 9–10; 13:1-3, 23-31). This remarkable cultural productivity was carried out by circles of a few dozen scribes, presumably mainly in Jerusalem, in service and support of the temple-state then at the head of a tiny Judean society in the area surrounding Jerusalem.

Meanwhile, the northern Israelites in Samaria and Galilee lived under separate rulers from the Judeans and from one another for many centuries. Under the Persian Empire and the successor Hellenistic imperial regimes, a local client aristocracy ruled over the Samaritans, who maintained their own temple and an alternative cult to the one in Jerusalem. In Galilee, under a separate imperial province, there is no evidence that a local aristocracy was ever imposed or developed. In both areas the cultivation of Israelite tradition presumably continued in the village communities, where local interaction was still presumably guided by Mosaic covenantal principles. There is no reason to believe, however, that ordinary Samaritans and Galileans were aware of the evolving "Scriptures" of the Judean temple-state.

Hasmonean Expansion and Its Effects

A new era dawned in the Israelite areas of Palestine with the rise of the Hasmonean high priesthood. In the early second century BCE, the tiny temple-state in Judea was headed by a priestly aristocracy subject to the Seleucid Empire, one of the successor kingdoms following the conquests of Alexander the Great. When the dominant faction in the priestly aristocracy, seeking to enhance their alliance with Emperor Antiochus IV "Epiphanes," attempted to transform Jerusalem into the Hellenistic city of "Antioch," several circles of scribal retainers resisted. They articulated their opposition to imperial rule and high priestly collaboration in several texts now classified as "apocalyptic" (see Daniel 7–12, the various "books" collected in *1 Enoch,* and the *Testament of Moses*).[4] More effective

---

4. See Horsley, *Scribes, Visionaries,* chapters 8 and 9; *Revolt of the Scribes: Resistance and Apocalyptic Origins* (Minneapolis: Fortress, 2010), chapters 1-5.

resistance, however, was mounted by Judean villagers in the 160s BCE under the leadership of the Hasmonean family, who became known as "the Maccabees" from the nickname of the charismatic leader of the "Maccabean" Revolt, Judas "the Hammer" *(maccabeus)*.

Within a decade or so after "the Maccabees" had fought the Seleucid armies to a standoff in a historic guerrilla war, the brothers of Judas, Jonathan and then Simon, negotiated with the Seleucid regime to set themselves up in a restored high priesthood in Jerusalem. Already in command of a strong army, the next two generations of Hasmonean high priests also hired Greek-speaking mercenary troops and systematically expanded their rule to include the territories that, according to Judean tradition, had been ruled by David and Solomon. John Hyrcanus, famous as the first Judean to hold the offices of both "king" and "high priest," captured and destroyed the city of Samaria along with Shechem and the Samaritan temple on Mount Gerizim (Josephus, *Antiquities* 13.154-56, 275, 280-81). In 104 BCE, Hyrcanus's son Aristobulus took control of Galilee and required the inhabitants to live according to "the laws of Judeans" (*Antiquities* 13.318-19). This must have meant yielding tithes and offerings to the temple and priesthood, since local interaction would have continued under local customs and Israelite (popular) tradition cultivated in village communities. Thus, after not having been under Jerusalem rule for over eight hundred years, the other principal areas of Israelite population, Samaria and Galilee, came under the Judean high priesthood a century before Jesus' birth.[5]

In Samaria, despite the destruction of the capital city and the temple on Mount Gerizim, some sort of aristocracy — Josephus variously calls them "the first ones" or "the powerful ones" — continued to have influence over and responsibility for the actions of the people (*Antiquities* 18.85-89; 20.118-36; *War* 2.239). In Galilee, however, where no ruling aristocracy had been imposed and none had emerged, the Hasmoneans and later Herod the Great established a more direct administrative apparatus consisting mainly of garrisoned fortresses in towns such as Sep-

---

5. For critical analysis of the sparse sources for the Hasmonean takeover of Samaria and Galilee and its implications, see Richard Horsley, *Galilee: History, Politics, People* (Harrisville: Trinity, 1995), chapter 2.

phoris (*War* 1.170, 304; 2.56). These would presumably have been staffed by Judean officers of the Hasmonean High Priest or Herod in Jerusalem. Considering the intense turmoil of pitched battles between rival Hasmoneans in the later decades of the dynasty and early decades of Roman rule it seems highly unlikely that the regime sent scribal retainers ("scribes and Pharisees") to carry out the "resocialization" of the Galileans that would have been necessary to replace local Israelite customs, laws, and traditions with law codes developed by scribes in Jerusalem (such as the Deuteronomic or Levitical codes).

The Judean officers and their military and administrative staff, however, some of whom must have succeeded their fathers in office, would have become a Judean layer of administrators resident in the garrisoned fortress towns, as often happens in such areas ruled from distant capital cities. Josephus provides some indication of the tense relations between the Judean officers of these installations and the local population. When Herod was struggling to gain control of Galilee after his appointment as king by the Romans in 40 BCE, Galilean mobs seized some of these "powerful ones" and "drowned them in the lake" (*Antiquities* 14.450; cf. *War* 1.326). These "powerful ones" would presumably have been Hasmonean officers who had shifted their allegiance to Herod after he was appointed king. Four decades later, in the revolt that erupted on word of Herod's death, a popularly acclaimed king — Judas, son of a brigand chieftain whom Herod had earlier killed — led a band of Galilean rebels against the royal fortress in Sepphoris and "took back the goods that had been taken there" (*Antiquities* 17.271). Tensions between the Galilean villagers and the officers and garrisons of Herod in Galilee had evidently continued through his reign.

The Regions of Israel at the Time of Jesus

Ironically it may be precisely these historical circumstances that are the roots from which arises the modern confusion of the Galileans and the Judeans as "Jews." Modern North Americans are familiar with the tendency of outside observers of the inhabitants of a nation to refer to them using the name of the dominant group of people. North Americans commonly refer to Great Britain or the United Kingdom as "England" and to the people who live there as "the English." Insiders, however, would distinguish clearly between the English and the Scots and the Welsh by regional provenance or continuing residence. It was similar in ancient Palestine. Having conquered the area after the Judean high priesthood had already taken over Samaria and Galilee, the Romans viewed much of Palestine as "Judea." When they appointed Herod as King, they gave him the title "King of the Judeans." Roman sources thus understandably refer to the inhabitants of or people from much of Palestine generally as "the Judeans," which became translated in English mainly as "the Jews."

According to Judean and other historical sources, however, insiders referred to the people of the different regions separately: those in (or from) Judea proper were "the Judeans," those in Samaria were "the Samaritans," and those in (or from) Galilee were "the Galileans." The Judean historian Josephus, in his extensive accounts of events and people in the early Roman period (in which he himself was involved), almost always uses the term *hoi Ioudaioi* ("the Judeans") in reference to people who live in Judea proper, often particularly for people in Jerusalem; he uses *hoi Galilaioi* ("the Galileans") for the people of Galilee, mainly in villages, and *hoi Samareis/Samareitai* ("the Samaritans") for inhabitants of Samaria.[6] The "outsiders'" (Romans, et al.) usage of *hoi Ioudaioi* as a general term for all of the people of Israelite heritage living in Palestine or in cities of the eastern Roman Empire became standard in biblical studies. Recent interpreters of the Gospel of Mark, for example, often refer to a "Jewish" side and a "Gentile" side of the Sea of Galilee, between which Jesus was supposedly mediating in his ministry. Except for Pontius Pilate's crucifixion of Jesus as "the king of the Judeans," however, the Gospel of Mark itself uses the term *hoi Ioudaioi* only once, clearly as a regional reference to "the Pharisees and all the (other) Judeans" in Jerusalem.[7]

6. See Sean Freyne, "Behind the Names Galileans, Samaritans, *Ioudaioi*," in *Galilee through the Centuries: Confluence of Cultures,* ed. Eric Meyers (Winona Lake: Eisenbrauns, 1999).

7. To maintain that the inhabitants of Galilee were *Ioudaioi* (Judeans/Jews) creates problems of historical explanation, leading scholars to hypothesize that the inhabitants

The people of all these regions together, Galileans, Samaritans, and Judeans, however, were referred to by "insiders" as "Israel/Israelites." In rabbinic texts, for example, the term of self-identification is "Israel/Israelite." One of the most accessible texts in which to see the difference between the outsiders' term of reference and the insiders' term comes in the crucifixion scene in Mark's Gospel. Pilate, the Roman governor of Judea, crucifies Jesus, who has come from Galilee, which is ruled by Herod Antipas, as "king of the Judeans" (15:26). When the high priests of the Judean temple-state mock Jesus on the cross, however, it is as "king of Israel" (v. 32).

One further usage of the term "the Judeans" in Josephus's historical accounts may help us when we turn eventually to examination of the Gospel of John. It is common in modern political parlance to use the name of an entire people group to refer narrowly to that group's government: "the Americans" for the United States government or administration in Washington, DC, or "the Chinese" for the government of China in Beijing. Josephus does somewhat the same thing when he explains (claiming to cite official Roman documents) that, after conquering Palestine, the Roman warlords granted to Hyrcanus and "the Judeans" rights to continue receiving the revenues of the areas they had previously controlled (*Antiquities* 14.205-9). Those revenues, however, were clearly going to the Hasmonean high priesthood, not to the general populace of Judea, much less of all the regions. Thus in Josephus's histories, while "the Judeans" refers generally to those who live in Judea (as distinguished from "the Samaritans" and "the Galileans"), the term often refers more particularly to the high priestly rulers of the Judeans in Jerusalem at the head of the temple-state.

Corresponding to the different regional terms by which our "insider" sources refer to the people of the different regions, there was considerable tension between these regions rooted in their different histories and particularly in the takeover of the Samaritans and Galileans by the rulers of the Judeans.

---

of Galilee underwent forced "conversion" at the hands of the Hasmonean high priesthood and/or that after the latter conquered the area in 104 BCE, there was a massive emigration of Judeans from Judea into Galilee. But neither of these hypothetical events is attested in our sources, and indeed the idea of a mass religious "conversion" is anachronistic.

The Galileans No Longer under Jerusalem Rule

Two results of the Roman decision to place Galilee under the rule of Herod Antipas following the revolt of 4 BCE are often overlooked in studies of the Gospels and Jesus. First, for the first time in the Israelite history of the region, the ruler of Galilee established his administration directly in the area, with obvious political-economic and cultural implications. Antipas's construction of two new cities — Sepphoris and Tiberias — in the first twenty years of his reign would have required extensive resources. Having nearly all the villages of lower Galilee within view from one or the other of these administrative centers, however, would have enhanced the "efficiency" of revenue collection. The impact was simultaneously cultural as well as economic. Antipas brought additional Judeans into his cities as military and administrative retainers and, having himself been raised in the imperial court in Rome, also brought an increase of Greco-Roman cultural influences. Among these were the increased use of Greek in the political-economic administration, the architecture and decor of "royal" and other public buildings in the cities, and the political-cultural orientation of the elite — all new and alien impositions on life in the traditional village communities. Not surprisingly, during the great revolt of 66-67 CE Galilean villagers were sharply hostile to Sepphoris and Tiberias, which remained loyal to the imperial regime in Rome. And it cannot be surprising that Galileans, offended by the decor in Antipas's palace in Tiberias, attacked the palace along with the capital city.

A second consequence of the Romans placing Galilee under Antipas's rule, of even greater import for understanding the Gospels and Jesus' mission, was the sudden removal of the Galileans from the political jurisdiction of the Judean temple and high priesthood. After being independent of Jerusalem rule for many centuries, then ruled and taxed from Jerusalem for a hundred years, during the lifetime of Jesus Galileans were again no longer under the direct rule of the temple-state.[8] Considering the turmoil of the Hasmonean regime during the sixty years it ruled Gali-

---

8. And thereafter until the destruction of the temple and the dismantling of its priesthood in 70 CE, except perhaps for the brief interlude under Agrippa I in 41-44 CE.

lee and Herod's subordination of the temple-state to his own rule for the next several decades, we may wonder what relationship the Galileans had with the temple and "the laws of the Judeans" that had been imposed on them.

It is often claimed that people living in Galilee went regularly to Jerusalem for the Passover and/or other pilgrimage festivals. This claim, like others, is rooted in the synthetic construct of "Judaism" in which "the Jews" are generally assumed to have taken part in festivals celebrated in the temple. The differences in regional history noted above, however, along with more practical considerations, resist such a claim. In contrast to Judean villagers, most of whom lived within fifteen miles of Jerusalem and whose families had five hundred years under the temple-state to acquire motives or habits of participating in temple festivals, Galileans had been under Jerusalem rule for only a century. Further, the distance and the time required for attendance at pilgrimage feasts were probably decisive: the journey would have taken several days each way, on top of the necessary purification period and the actual time spent at the festival itself. Villagers who worked the soil for their own food and payment of taxes, tribute, and tithes could hardly have taken that amount of time away from agricultural labor. It is difficult to imagine that most Galileans went to Jerusalem for festivals on a regular basis.[9]

It is also claimed that the people of Galilee knew and practiced the

---

9. For further discussion see Horsley, *Galilee,* 144-47. An incident recorded by Josephus has often been cited as evidence for widespread pilgrimage by Galileans to Jerusalem for festivals, yet the varying accounts of this episode make a definitive reconstruction of the event difficult. "It was the custom of the Galileans at the time of a festival to pass through the Samaritan territory on their way to the Holy City. On one occasion [some Samaritan villagers] slew a great number of them" (*Antiquities* 20.118). Strangely, however, the incidents that follow involved a sustained conflict between Samaritans and Judeans. Moreover, the account in *War* (2.232-37) twice states that only "a certain [= single] Galilean" traveling in "a large company of Judeans" was killed (*War* 2.232, 237), perhaps envisioning Judeans living and working in Galilee who were returning home for the festival. The situation is further complicated by the fact that Tacitus, commenting on the same sequence of events, portrays the rival Samaritan and Galilean factions as bandit privateers, not as religious pilgrims (*Annals* 12.54). Perhaps most significant is the fact that Josephus clearly and sharply distinguishes between "Galileans," "Samaritans," and "Judeans."

written Law/Torah promoted by the Judean priesthood and scribes. As noted in chapter 1, however, Galileans would presumably have cultivated their Israelite popular tradition with whatever distinctive regional twists it may have developed during the centuries under regimes different from those that ruled the Jerusalem temple-state. Thus, for example, incidents involving Galileans' actions against Herodians and others during the great revolt in 66-67 CE indicate not attachment to authoritative books but a commitment to the basic commandments of the Mosaic covenant.[10] Josephus's account of the Hasmonean takeover in Galilee mentions simply that the Galileans were forced to accept "the laws of the Judeans," most likely regulations regarding tithes and offerings and other matters pertaining to the relationship between rulers and ruled. It is difficult to imagine that "the (written) Torah of Moses" was pressed on the Galileans during the century of Jerusalem rule, for a number of interrelated reasons. Written texts of Torah, such as the books of the Pentateuch in the archaic literary language of Hebrew, were cultivated mainly in scribal circles. Even if they had been available in the ordinary people's language of Aramaic, the non-literate people of Galilee could not have read them. In late second temple times in Jerusalem, the books of the Pentateuch were authoritative in Jerusalem, but that authority was relative, for example, to the regulations derived from the traditions of the ancestors by the Pharisees that were included in state law, depending on the incumbent high priest (see, e.g., *Antiquities* 13.297-98, 408). Josephus, like the earlier learned scribe Ben Sira, represents the scribes and Pharisees as based in and working in Jerusalem. Other than the references in the Gospel of Mark to their having "come down from Jerusalem" (3:22; 7:1-2), there are simply no references to Jerusalem scribes and Pharisees appearing in Galilean villages, or even in Judean villages for that matter, and Mark shows the Pharisees coming not to teach the people but to dispute with Jesus. Overall, although they probably knew of the existence of the sacred books of the Jerusalem temple-state, it is difficult to imagine that Galilean villagers were attached to the written books of Torah.[11]

10. Critical analysis and discussion of Josephus's accounts are in Horsley, *Galilee,* 152-55.

11. See further Horsley, *Galilee,* 149-52.

The Samaritans under Jerusalem and Roman Rule

In Israelite tradition, the conflict between Samaria and Jerusalem was rooted in Solomon's subjection of Israelites to forced labor and, after the break, the northern Israelite kingdom's establishment of alternative sacrifices to God. Under the Persian Empire and the early Hellenistic empires, the priestly aristocracies of Jerusalem and Samaria engaged in repeated conflicts for imperial favor, each claiming to represent proper and legitimate worship of their common God (Ezra 4:1–5:5; *Antiquities* 11.114-19; 12.257-64). The Hasmonean conquest and destruction of Samaria and the temple on Mount Gerizim struck a decisive blow to the Samaritan aristocracy. Under Roman rule, the latter played a minor role compared to that of the priestly aristocracy in Jerusalem (*Antiquities* 18.85-89; 20.118-36).

The Samaritans' resentment of Jerusalem and Judean dominance extended to the villagers as well, as evident from two major incidents recounted by Josephus. Just after Rome had placed Judea under the oversight of a governor in 6 CE, some Samaritans, entering Jerusalem secretly at the festival of Passover, scattered human bones in the porticoes and through the whole temple courtyard (*Antiquities* 18.30), thus rendering the area utterly impure. This was a sacrilege against the temple, to be sure, but it was also a calculated act of protest against the political power centralized in the hands of the Judean priestly rulers in Jerusalem.

Indicative of how widespread and deep-seated tension between Judeans and Samaritans were is the incident in the late 40s CE that began with the murder of (a) Galilean(s) en route to Jerusalem on the northern border of Samaria. The murder escalated into a major conflict between the Samaritans and the Judeans that quickly involved the respective aristocracies as well as attacks by Judeans on the Samaritans, punitive action by the governor Cumanus, and eventually a hearing over what became a major disruption of the Roman imperial order in Palestine (*War* 2.232-49; *Antiquities* 18.118-36). In the account in *Antiquities*, Josephus has a crowd of Galileans ready to retaliate, and in both *Antiquities* and *War* "the principal men of the Galileans" (notables of the city of Sepphoris?) appeal to Cumanus, whose jurisdiction included western Galilee, to intervene. According to *Antiquities*, when news of the murder reached Jerusalem a crowd led by the brigand chieftain Eleazar ben Dinai rushed off to attack Samaritan villagers; according to *War,* some Galileans urged the mass of Judeans "to resort to arms to assert their liberty *(eleutheria),*" suggesting that this matter somehow concerned the Judean subjugation to Rome. For their part, the "rulers/officers of the Judeans" (the high priests) implored the angry Judean mob not to take action, since it would bring down the wrath of the Romans on Jerusalem and the temple. Forced into action to quell the escalating disturbance, Cumanus intervened with troops from Sebaste on the side of the Samaritans and slew many of the Judean attackers and took many others prisoner, which only led to further local raids and insurrections around the Judean countryside.

The Samaritan aristocracy appealed to Ummidius Quadratus, legate of Syria (the Roman officer above Cumanus) to intervene. Upon investigation he crucified both the Judeans and the Samaritans whom Cumanus had taken prisoner, and on further information from a Samaritan he had several other purported leaders of the Judean attackers put to death. Quadratus then sent the high priests Jonathan and Ananias, the temple captain Ananus, and several other Judean (priestly) rulers in chains, along with the Samaritan aristocrats, to render account of themselves to the emperor Claudius. He also sent Cumanus and the military tribune Celer off to Rome for trial before Caesar. In an illustration of how the imperial system worked, Herod Agrippa the younger, later to be named king of eastern Galilee and Gaulanitis, intervened through the emperor's wife Agrippina to influence Claudius to decide in favor of the Judean high priests. The emperor ordered three of the Samaritan aristocrats executed, banished Cumanus, and sent Celer back in chains to Jerusalem to be dragged around the city and executed.

This steadily escalating conflict between the Samaritans and the Judeans is a classic illustration of how well "divide and conquer" can work as a strategy of imperial control of subject peoples. Since it was simply suicidal to direct resentment and violence upward against the Romans, they became diverted into fratricidal strife and occasional overt conflict.

While these two incidents, one in the first decade of the first century CE and the other in the fifth, vividly illustrate the acute tension between

Samaritans and Judeans, it is important to recognize that both were Israelite peoples who cultivated Israelite cultural traditions. This is illustrated by the common pattern of the popular prophetic movements that occurred in Samaria as well as in Judea right around the time of the mission of Jesus of Nazareth. The movement led up Mount Gerizim by a prophet in Samaria, like the one led by Theudas in Judea, was patterned after Israelite tradition of the founding prophet Moses that was clearly cultivated among Samaritan as well as among Judean and Galilean villagers.

The Samaritans, the Galileans, and the Judeans were all Israelites living from the same Israelite cultural tradition. The different regional histories, however, particularly the long period of Galilean and Samaritan independence from Jerusalem rule followed by subjection to it, had complicated and compounded the basic division between rulers and ruled, between the priestly aristocracy of Jerusalem appointed by the Romans and (particularly) the Galilean and Samaritan as well as the Judean villagers.

The Renewal of Israel

The deep longing of Israelites for a renewal of their society, a longing that undergirded their persistent resistance to Roman and Jerusalem rule, was firmly rooted in shared Israelite tradition. The several movements of resistance reviewed in chapter 1 were also movements of renewal. More striking, perhaps because we might not expect scribal retainers to have been so sharply opposed to the rulers on whom their own positions depended, the focal concern in Judean "apocalyptic" texts was on the restoration of Israel that would follow the termination of oppressive imperial rule.

The yearning for liberation and the restoration of the people in their ancestral land had long been articulated by Israel's prophets. Particularly prominent, and perhaps particularly influential, were the prophecies that now appear in the book of Isaiah, which anticipate God's defeat of the imperial regime that had conquered the people and look to a return to independence. The metaphors and hyperboles that Isaiah uses to describe God's terrifying appearance to defeat and deliver have sometimes been mistaken (in overly literal readings) as predictions of the "end of the world" (e.g., Isaiah 13). Statements such as "your dead shall live, their corpses shall rise" (Isa 26:19) have been taken as references to an eschatological resurrection of the dead rather than a restoration of the people. And the hyperbole of "a new heaven and new earth" has similarly been read too literally and taken out of its context, where it refers to the restoration of the people on their land without the attacks and exploitation of foreign rulers (Isa 65:17-25). Images of a new exodus, the reassembly or restoration of the twelve tribes, and a renewed covenant are particularly prominent (e.g., Isaiah 40–55; Jeremiah 31). This rich tradition underlies the popular longing for "freedom" *(eleutheria),* a life under the rule of God, to which Josephus refers frequently in his histories of life under Roman rule. That this "freedom" meant political independence, not just "freedom of religion," is indicated by Josephus's use of the term *palingenesia.* Exegesis and translation of Matt 19:28 has often taken this as a reference to the "regeneration" of the cosmos, as in Stoic philosophy. But it is clear in Josephus's usage that in the context of Roman rule in Palestine, it meant the restoration of the twelve tribes of Israel on their land (*Antiquities* 11.66, 107).[12]

Evidence for the scribal agenda of restoration is both explicit and extensive in late second temple Judean texts. Much of this evidence has been missed or misread because the sources have been read through yet another synthetic scholarly construct, that of "apocalypticism." As articulated by influential scholars such as Albert Schweitzer and Rudolf Bultmann in the early twentieth century, these texts were taken as focused on the end of the world in a "cosmic catastrophe," an apocalyptic scenario that included the imminent Time of Tribulation and the Son of Man coming in the Last Judgment. In fact, the "apocalyptic" texts themselves say nothing of the sort. They are rather concerned to understand the historical crisis posed by the invasion of Jerusalem by imperial armies to forcibly interfere with the traditional Israelite way of life. At the end of these texts' reviews of history, they project eager hope for the resolution of the crisis in God's judgment of the foreign empire and restora-

---

12. See further Richard Horsley, *Jesus and the Spiral of Violence: Popular Jewish Resistance in Roman Palestine* (San Francisco: Harper & Row, 1987), 202-3.

tion of his people, sometimes on a renewed earth under restored heavenly governance.[13]

In the best known apocalyptic texts, the historical visions and interpretations in Daniel 7 and 10–12, the focus on the end of empire and the restoration of the people to sovereignty could not be clearer. "The one like a human being coming with the clouds of heaven" who was "given dominion and kingship" (7:13-14) is interpreted as "the people of the holy ones of the Most High" — that is, the people of Judea/Israel, who regain their independence under God after the termination of the invasive and oppressive Hellenistic empires (vv. 18, 27). The future described briefly at the end of the review of history in Daniel 10–12 is, again, the deliverance of the people, of which the resurrection and the vindication of the "wise" martyrs for their faithful resistance are components (12:1-3). In some of the Judean texts that were collected in the composite *1 Enoch,* which, like the visions and interpretations in Daniel 7–12, were influential in late second temple scribal circles, the vision of the future is more elaborate. In the Animal Vision (*1 Enoch* 85–90), which denigrates the second temple built under imperial rule as polluted, the people will be restored on the land in a great "house" (of God), but the restored house is pointedly to be without a "tower," that is, without the temple (89:73; 90:29). Closer to the time of Jesus, in the Similitudes of Enoch (*1 Enoch* 37–69), after "the kings and the mighty" face divine judgment, the people of Israel will be restored on a restored earth.[14]

Also closer to the time of Jesus, in response to Roman imperial rule, the non-apocalyptic scribal text *Psalms of Solomon* 17 looks for God, through his agent the anointed Son of David, to restore the twelve tribes in their land in a life of justice. The scribes and priests who, led by the Moses-like "righteous teacher," launched a new exodus into the wilderness of Judea at Qumran, did not wait for God to act, but established a re-

13. See the analysis of the texts in Horsley, *Revolt of the Scribes,* along with the critique of the "apocalyptic scenario" of the "end of the world" articulated by Schweitzer and Bultmann that became the standard view of apocalypticism in interpretation of the Gospels and Jesus in Horsley, *The Prophet Jesus and the Renewal of Israel* (Grand Rapids: Eerdmans, 2012), chapters 1-5.

14. For critical analysis and discussion of the texts, see Horsley, *Scribes, Visionaries,* chapters 8 and 9; *Revolt of the Scribes,* chapters 4, 5, and 9.

newed covenant community of Israel under the representative figures of "twelve men and three priests," who were charged with effecting justice and loving kindness and preserving faith in the land (1QS 8.1-4).

Given the divide between scribal culture and village culture, the scribal texts noted above may not be taken as direct sources for the attitudes of ordinary people. But if opposition to the imperial and Jerusalem rulers and hope for renewal of the people were strong at least in some scribal circles, it is not surprising that they would be even more widespread among ordinary Israelites. In fact, the longing for freedom was sufficiently intense among Israelite villagers that they formed several movements that attempted to realize the renewal of Israel, as noted briefly in chapter 1. These movements, moreover, took forms that were distinctive to Israelite tradition: messianic movements patterned after the young David's leadership of the people in reestablishing their independent life and prophetic movements patterned after Moses and Joshua leading Israel in the exodus and into independence on their land. While these movements have been recognized as forms of resistance to Roman rule, they were also movements of renewal, judging from Josephus's accounts.

The messianic movements in 4 BCE succeeded in establishing the people's independence and self-governance (without rule from above by either Jerusalem or Rome) for several months or, in the movement led by the shepherd Athronges in northwest Judean villages, for nearly three years (*War* 2.56-76; *Antiquities* 17.271-92). During the great revolt of 66-70, the popularly acclaimed king Simon bar Giora implemented a social-economic program of cancellation of debts and, in effect, "land reform," evidently restoring families to their ancestral lands (*War* 2.652-53; 4.503-13). The messianic movements were clearly more than simply revolts led by populist kings. And it is surely significant that these movements did not take place only in Judea. In 4 BCE, just about the time Jesus was born, the movement led by the brigand chief Judas son of Hezekiah operated in and around Sepphoris, near Nazareth, in Galilee. And another movement emerged in the Transjordan, another area of Israelite heritage.

Similarly, the people who participated in prophetic movements were looking for more than some fantastic act of God like one of the acts of old in early Israelite legends (*Antiquities* 20.97-98, 169-71; *War* 2.261-63). The procession into the wilderness led by Theudas evidently anticipated a new entry into the land, somehow freed of rule and exploitation. Likewise, the procession up to the Mount of Olives led by the "Egyptian" prophet to witness the collapse of the walls of Jerusalem and the disappearance of the Roman soldiers must have anticipated a life of freedom in the land once the ruling city had collapsed like Jericho of old. Again, the prophetic movements were not confined to Judea. As noted just above, one of the best known was in Samaria. Insofar as Josephus's account of this incident makes it seem less fantastic than the others, it may give us a better sense of how the prophets and their followers were looking for a renewed society under God. The Samaritan prophet led a sizeable band up to Mount Gerizim, the sacred mountain of the Samaritans, where their temple had stood before being destroyed by the Judean High Priest Hyrcanus. "He assured them that on their arrival he would show them the sacred vessels which were buried there, where Moses had deposited them" (*Antiquities* 18.85-87). This detail suggests that they were looking for a life like that of newly formed Israel in Moses' time, gathered around the tabernacle and free of rule from a temple and aristocracy, as well as from imperial overlords.

Anticipating a fresh reading of the Gospel accounts of Jesus' mission, it may be important to highlight a particular aspect of these texts and movements of renewal of Israel. It seems clear from the popular movements that they were attempting to realize a life free of rule from the Jerusalem temple-state as well as independent of Roman rule. It may come as a surprise that the scribes who produced apocalyptic texts also looked for a restored Israel that did not have a temple. This is striking for texts produced by circles of scribes whose role had been to advise and assist in the administration of the temple-state. When their high priestly patrons collaborated closely in imperial rule, however, some scribes insisted on the ideals in the Israelite tradition of a more just society free of oppressive rulers.

Earlier readings of apocalyptic texts claimed that they anticipated a rebuilt temple in the new age.[15] But that is simply not the case.[16] The vi-

---

15. Particularly influential with regard to the revival of "historical Jesus" studies has been E. P. Sanders, *Jesus and Judaism* (Philadelphia: Fortress, 1985), chapters 2 and 3.

16. Fuller analysis and discussion of the key texts are in Horsley, *Jesus and the Spiral*, especially 289-91; *Scribes, Visionaries*, chapters 8 and 9; and *Revolt of the Scribes*, chapters 4, 5, 7, and 8.

sions and interpretations in Daniel do not mention a temple in the restoration of the people. Nor does the oracle of glorious renewal in the *Testament of Moses* 10. The Animal Vision in *1 Enoch* 85-90 states pointedly that the temple was polluted, and it mentions no temple ("tower") in the rebuilding of the "house" that represents the renewal of Israel.

It is likely that all the various circles of dissident scribes that produced the apocalyptic texts and Qumran texts still comprised a minority of the scribal retainers. According to Josephus, "the leading Pharisees" continued to work with the high priests during the great revolt and surely did so during the preceding decades. It is nevertheless significant that several circles of dissident scribes, and not simply those who led the "Fourth Philosophy" and the "Sicarii," were evidently opposed to the incumbent high priestly rulers. They looked for God's judgment of invasive imperial rule to be followed by a restoration of the people without the temple-state. And if even some scribes who were dependent on the priestly rulers looked for the renewal of the people in independence of the temple-state, how much more would the Israelite villagers of the various regions.

The Gospels as Stories and Sources

CHAPTER THREE

Taking the Gospels Whole

Recent interpretation of Jesus has focused mostly on his individual sayings. While Johannine scholars have sometimes complained that the Fourth Gospel has been overlooked in preference for the Synoptics, the focus has been less against John than in favor of the sayings in the Synoptic Gospel tradition, the large majority of which find no parallel in the Fourth Gospel. This focus is rooted both in Christian theology and in the modern scientific stance toward the Gospel narratives.

Reformation and early modern theology prided itself on being scripturally based. Every doctrine was supported by citations of individual statements from Scripture. This was correlated with and supported by the form given to the Scriptures in modern translations such as the King James Version and the Lutherbibel, in which each verse was printed as a separate sentence coded by chapter and verse. This format facilitated the citation of authoritative statements as proof-texts for the various doctrines of Christology, soteriology, and ecclesiology. The Gospels in particular were treated as containers in which the sayings of Jesus or statements about Jesus or stories about Jesus were collected. Theologians and biblical scholars in particular developed a deeply ingrained habit of focusing on one verse at a time, particularly on the sayings of Jesus, which were deemed particularly authoritative.

Under the influence of Enlightenment reason and the scientific worldview, many interpreters found it difficult to take literally or even seriously narratives such as "miracle" stories or birth narratives or resurrection stories, which involved supernatural causation and/or otherworldly creatures such as angels. The only part of the Synoptic tradition that seemed to provide an acceptable basis for modern rational interpretation of Jesus was his teaching, appropriated in the form of individual sayings.

The focus on the individual sayings of Jesus was further reinforced by the recognition that the Gospels contained statements of "post-Easter" faith about Jesus as distinguished from what Jesus himself may have said or done. Discovery of the divide between the "historical" Jesus prior to the resurrection and the "Christ of faith" led to skepticism about the reliability of the Gospel narratives, on the one hand, and attention to the particular theologies articulated in the respective Gospels, on the other. But the Gospels were still viewed and interpreted as containers of separate sayings of Jesus, statements about Jesus, and scriptural lessons. Since the principal purpose of interpretation of the Gospels remained appreciation and explication of the teaching of Jesus, the focus remained on the individual sayings.

The result in New Testament studies has been that interpretation of Jesus, whether presented as "the historical Jesus" or as Jesus represented in a particular Gospel, has tended to focus on his sayings. In the revival of interest in the historical Jesus in the late twentieth century it has simply been assumed that interpretation proceeds by focusing on individual sayings of Jesus. The standard approach has been to isolate individual sayings of Jesus from their literary contexts, classify them by form and/or content, establish their original or early wording, and assess their authenticity. Finally, on the assumption that separate individual sayings had meaning in themselves, scholars sought to establish that meaning.[1] A further operating assumption in highly individualistic modern Western biblical studies was that Jesus uttered separate sayings to individuals, who then remembered them and transmitted them to other individ-

---

1. The most sophisticated critical development of this approach is John Dominic Crossan, *The Historical Jesus: The Life of a Mediterranean Jewish Peasant* (San Francisco: HarperCollins, 1991).

uals until someone "collected" them — and "stabilized" their wording — by "writing" a Gospel. The Synoptic Gospels Matthew, Mark, and Luke appeared to interpreters as collections of individual sayings and assessable anecdotes with particular adaptations, twists, and juxtapositions. Thus, interpretation of the view of Jesus in particular Gospels, like interpretation of the historical Jesus, focused on the individual sayings of Jesus — as attested in any number of commentaries on the Gospels, in which interpretation proceeded in the long-standardized verse-by-verse format.

Recovering the Gospels as Stories

Several decades ago, however, as interpreters of Jesus were continuing to refine their focus on individual sayings, Gospel interpreters began exploring new theoretical models of literary criticism and various aspects of ancient communications culture (the technologies by which ideas were shaped and communicated in antiquity). This new research proceeded more or less separately in several interrelated areas — including studies of orality and literacy, textual criticism, and social memory — while the new narrative criticism of the Gospels took its inspiration from modern literary criticism and its assumptions about modern prose fiction. It is now becoming evident, however, that the implications of these various explorations reinforce one another in challenging what had become standard assumptions and procedures in interpretation of the Gospels and investigation of the historical Jesus. We can focus here on only a few of the more basic ways in which these consensus assumptions have been problematized.

First, there turns out to be no basis on which the "original" saying or even a fixed "early" form of a Jesus saying can be established. This was the goal of form criticism, which came to prominence early in the last century and was developed into an even more sophisticated procedure by the liberal interpreters of the Jesus Seminar in the 1980s. A prime candidate for this procedure would be a saying that has "multiple attestation," such as Jesus' saying that "a prophet has no honor," which appears in all four canonical Gospels (Matt 13:57; Mark 6:4; Luke 4:24; John 4:44) and the Gospel of Thomas (31:1). On the assumption that the Gospels were all "written" by individual "authors," the first step was to establish, by comparing the ancient manuscripts of each Gospel, the "original" wording or form of the saying in each Evangelist's "autograph." By comparing the versions in the five different Gospels, scholars would reason backward through Matthew's and Luke's adaptations of Mark's version and then speculate on the processes of oral transmission behind the versions in Mark, John, and Thomas; these reflections, in turn, led to speculation on the "original" or "early" form of this saying of Jesus. Interpreters would then attempt to discern the "original" meaning of the saying by recontextualizing it in their own respective hypothetical reconstructions of Jesus' world and career. Following this model, the "meaning" of the "prophet has no honor" saying is established by comparing its original meaning to Mark's or John's interpretations of it.

New research into oral communications culture and its interface with writing in antiquity first exposed how problematic this procedure was. In his pioneering investigation of how oral tradition works, Werner Kelber demonstrated that form criticism was grounded in a model of "tradition" that understood the oral transmission of Jesus' sayings by analogy with Matthew and Luke's adaptations of the written text of Mark.[2] But proceeding from research on the ways that oral traditions work in a predominantly oral culture, it would be utterly impossible to establish an "original" form of particular sayings, which would have been multiform in the oral communications process.

Kelber's groundbreaking insight is now powerfully reinforced by recent text-critical work on the earliest manuscripts of the Gospels. It had been recognized for some time that the carefully established Greek text of the Gospels on which modern translations are based and from which scholars work is the product of modern text criticism. In fact, the very idea that there was an establishable "original" or early text is derived from modern print culture, where one can readily compare minute details between carefully edited, machine-produced documents. But recent investigation of the available ancient manuscripts, including fragments, is now

---

2. Werner H. Kelber, *The Oral and the Written Gospel* (Philadelphia: Fortress, 1983), chapter 1.

showing that the process of textual copying and transmission was fluid and dynamic in the second and third centuries, more akin to the workings of orality than to modern conventions of "copying." Some sort of standardization began only in the fourth and fifth centuries, partly under the influence of the imperial establishment of Christianity under Constantine. Especially challenging to the focus on individual sayings of Jesus, particularly the notion that early forms of individual sayings should serve as the primary "data" for historical reconstruction, are the findings of text critic David Parker.[3] Parker demonstrates that variation among early manuscripts of the Gospels is in fact greatest for sayings that were of particular importance for ongoing community life. Evidently, the teachings of Jesus that began in multiformity (he said similar things in different ways on multiple occasions) in the earliest communities of Jesus' followers continued to be multiform even after the wording of those teachings was committed to writing. Recent text criticism has thus decisively reinforced the insight that there is no basis in either the ancient manuscripts or oral tradition for the procedure of focusing on individual sayings and finding their "original" or early forms.[4]

Second, the focus on individual sayings ignores the communication process that would have been necessary for Jesus to become an important historical figure in the first place. Interpreters of Jesus and the Gospels conceive of Jesus as having uttered "aphorisms" and "pithy sayings" that were then transmitted from one individual to another, as if in an ancient version of the game of "telephone." But people cannot *communicate* in isolated individual sayings — no one speaks only in "one-liners." Jesus must have communicated and interacted with other people who resonated with his speech and action in the contexts of their own lives. Like fragments of pottery in museum cases, the isolated individual sayings of Jesus may be precious artifacts to the scholars who sort them out and categorize them, but since they cannot have been units of meaningful communication between Jesus and other people, they are not by themselves

---

3. David Parker, *The Living Text of the Gospels* (Cambridge: Cambridge University Press, 1997).

4. See especially Werner Kelber, "Jesus and Tradition: Words in Time, Words in Space," pages 139-67 in *Orality and Textuality in Early Christian Literature,* ed. Joanna Dewey (Semeia Studies; Atlanta: Scholars, 1995), 51.

historical sources for Jesus. And these tiny fragments of text cannot, by themselves, convey "meaning" in a sense that would assist in interpretation of the larger Gospels in which they appear.

Third, the focus on individual sayings and anecdotes, whether as statements of theology or as the sources for the historical Jesus, ignores the actual literary form of the Gospels. While it has gone largely ignored by interpreters of the historical Jesus, other New Testament scholars have developed an ever more critical understanding of the Gospels as whole stories. Almost simultaneously, about forty years ago, both theologians and biblical scholars (re-)discovered narrative, part of the discovery of the importance of story in the wider culture. Theologian Hans Frei articulated an influential criticism that the biblical narratives had been "eclipsed" by their contents.[5] Individual sayings and scenes from the Gospels, quite apart from their broader narrative context, were taken as windows onto events and incidents to which they referred, from which interpreters (re)constructed the history or historical contexts in which those sayings and scenes were then interpreted. The Gospels, the literary frameworks in which sayings and scenes are embedded, were ignored or dismissed as mere containers or collections or "strings of beads."

Concurrently, and well before the current wave of investigation of the historical Jesus gained momentum, an increasing number of New Testament scholars were (re-)discovering the literary integrity of the Gospels as whole stories about Jesus' mission in interactive speech and action.[6] Perhaps most important was the recognition that the Gospels were sustained narratives comprised of many episodes that were components of the developing story and intelligible only in the broader context of the whole story. The Gospels, moreover, were not just one episode

5. Hans Frei, *The Eclipse of Biblical Narrative: A Study in Eighteenth and Nineteenth Century Hermeneutics* (New Haven: Yale University Press, 1974).

6. Influential early analyses include Werner H. Kelber, *Mark's Story of Jesus* (Philadelphia: Fortress, 1979); David Rhoads and Donald Michie, *Mark as Story: An Introduction to the Narrative of a Gospel* (Philadelphia: Fortress, 1982); and R. Alan Culpepper, *Anatomy of the Fourth Gospel: A Study in Literary Design* (Philadelphia: Fortress, 1983). Critical review of literary-critical readings of the whole Gospel stories are in Stephen D. Moore, *Literary Criticism and the Gospels: The Theoretical Challenge* (New Haven: Yale University Press, 1989).

after another, but were stories with overall plots, in which earlier episodes and events both set up and led to subsequent episodes and events.

The Gospels as Historical Stories

One of the most fundamental responsibilities of biblical scholars, like that of historians, is to assess critically the character of their sources. Once a text is recognized as a psalm of praise or a prayer of confession or a letter from an apostle to a particular community, it would only fragment and distort that text to tear a particular "verse" or statement out of its literary and social contexts and treat it as if it had some meaning in itself apart from the text of which it was/is a component. Historians would not separate individual sentences or short anecdotes from their historical sources, categorize them by key words or apparent topics, and then look for the meaning of each statement in isolation. Particular sentences are intelligible only in literary context in relation to arguments or explanations. Anecdotes make sense only in narrative context or as illustrations of arguments or circumstances. To establish the "authenticity" or even the "meaning" of isolated sayings or anecdotes is difficult in the extreme, since they are embedded in the rhetoric of the sources. Modern historians thus generally begin by assessing their sources in their literary integrity (considering the dynamics of the whole) and then proceed to consider how they can be used as historical sources.

The recognition that the Gospels are sustained narratives, whole stories of Jesus' mission, and that their individual parts are shaped by and meaningful only within their current literary contexts is thus a crucial step from which there is no going back to a focus on the tiny text-fragments of sayings and scenes. The latter can only be understood as episodes in a larger story. The Gospels as whole stories, and not the individual sayings and anecdotes, are the sources for our understanding of Jesus in historical context. For interpretation of Jesus, therefore, it is necessary to "back up," as it were, and, rather than ignoring or bypassing the Gospel stories, first to understand them and then move *through* them to Jesus-in-context.

The first step in understanding the Gospels as stories and using them as sources is thus to gain an appreciation of the stories they tell. Only after gaining a sense of the stories can we then focus their respective portrayals of Jesus' mission. While the Gospels all tell more or less the same basic story, they are different in significant ways. Mark offers a largely rapid-fire narrative in which one brief episode leads to another and all move toward the climactic events, pausing twice along the way for speeches of Jesus. Matthew and Luke follow Mark's narrative, but Luke inserts shorter or much longer blocks of Jesus' teachings while Matthew takes five breaks in the action for speeches of Jesus on particular concerns. John's story proceeds in a series of actions intertwined with dialogues and monologues with a long speech by Jesus before the climactic events. All the Gospels are plotted sustained narratives.

In the first flush of the (re-)discovery of narrative nearly a generation ago, Gospel interpreters took many cues from criticism of modern narrative fiction, reading these ancient narratives like modern novels or short stories. Particularly influential were structuralist theories that tended to treat stories as closed semiotic systems, rhetorical acts of communication between their (implied) authors, narrators, and (implied) readers. Composition of the Gospels and their relationships to the ancient historical social or cultural context were deferred and, in many cases, dismissed as irrelevant. The structuralist approach and "reader-response" criticism located the "meaning" of the Gospel narratives squarely in the texts themselves or in the social locations of their modern readers, without reference to the experiences and lifeways of the Evangelists or their ancient audiences.[7] The structuralist approach and "reader-response" criticism allowed the meaning of the Gospel narrative to be discovered in the mind of the reader.

Ancient stories, however, are different from modern novellas in significant ways. For example, the plots of the Gospels are not linear and do

---

7. Such narrative-critical approaches left an indelible mark on Johannine Studies in the 1980s and 1990s; recent interpretation has taken a more balanced approach, as evident, for example, in the reflective essays by leading Johannine scholars in Tom Thatcher, ed., *What We Have Heard from the Beginning: The Past, Present, and Future of Johannine Studies* (Waco: Baylor University Press, 2007). See particularly the essays by John Ashton, Johannes Beutler, Alan Culpepper, Robert Kysar, Francis Moloney, and Moody Smith.

not generate suspense — the outcome of the story is anticipated all along, apparently under the assumption that the audience already knows what happens at the end. The characters in the Gospels are types, even stereotypes, playing important roles but not undergoing "character development." The Gospel stories are simply not comparable to modern fiction. They present themselves as historical stories about a powerfully significant person of vivid recent memory, and they present him not only as a life-changing figure but as a person who changed history. The Gospel stories are embedded in and repeatedly reference Israelite tradition and present Jesus as its fulfillment. They virtually insist on being understood not only in a particular historical-cultural context but also in a particular historical-political context as well. It is thus only appropriate to the Gospels to attempt to analyze and appreciate these historical stories in historical context.[8]

As the first step in understanding the Gospels themselves and possibly using them as sources for Jesus, it is thus necessary to *take the Gospel stories whole, and then to focus on their overall portrayal of Jesus' mission in interaction with followers and with the rulers of the people in the circumstances of the historical setting.* While recognizing that ancient stories are different from modern prose fiction in significant ways, it may be helpful to begin analysis with some of the fundamental questions asked of stories in Literature 101 courses: setting, principal characters, and plot. While these elements are inseparable in the stories themselves, it may help analytically to gain a sense of each, particularly the plot, in an effort to appreciate the Gospel stories as they unfold.

Consensus seems to be holding that the Gospel of Mark was the first story of Jesus to be composed, with the other "Synoptic" Gospels, Matthew and Luke, basically following Mark's story. Although there is less of a consensus about the "source" of the (non-Markan) teachings of Jesus that are strikingly parallel in Matthew and Luke, it is clear that both of these Gospels drew on some source, oral and/or written, that included blocks of Jesus' teaching, a source commonly referred to as "Q" (short for

---

8. Earlier attempts to combine narrative and historical analysis include Ched Myers, *Binding the Strong Man* (Maryknoll: Orbis, 1988), and Richard Horsley, *Hearing the Whole Story* (Louisville: Westminster John Knox, 2001).

German *Quelle,* "source"). Mark and "Q" have been taken as the earliest Gospel texts and, hence, the most important for interpretation of the historical Jesus. In the world of biblical scholarship, the Gospel of Mark is perhaps the most intensively investigated story of Jesus, and the composition of Q has recently been closely analyzed as well. Mark's story and the series of speeches in the source drawn on by both Matthew and Luke have also been well explored from the perspective of ancient communications media, such as oral performance. We therefore begin our consideration of whole stories of Jesus' mission and speeches with a survey of the portrayals in Mark and Q, using this discussion to lay a conceptual and methodological foundation for our reading of the Gospel of John in later chapters.[9]

The Gospel of Mark: Plotting Renewal

To enhance appreciation of the Gospels as stories, we strongly urge readers, before continuing with the following sketch of Mark's story, to read quickly through the Gospel, twice or more if possible, preferably in a format without chapter and verse numbers and especially without editorial subtitles, which are often misleading and break the flow of the narrative.[10]

The Gospel of Mark is set in Roman Palestine. Jesus proclaims the kingdom of God and performs healings and exorcisms mainly in the villages of Galilee for much of the story, with a few moves beyond the frontier into the villages in areas to the north and east. While in Galilee, Jesus and his disciples never venture into the capital cities. The climactic events of the story, however, take place in Jerusalem, where Jesus engages in a sustained confrontation with the rulers in the temple. Yet at

9. For more extensive analysis, see Horsley, *Hearing the Whole Story,* chapters 1, 4, and 5; "Q and Jesus: Assumptions, Approaches, and Analyses," *Semeia* 55 (1991), 175-209; Horsley with Jonathan A. Draper, *Whoever Hears You Hears Me: Prophets, Performance and Tradition in Q* (Harrisburg: Trinity, 1999), especially chapters 4 and 9-13.

10. To gain a sense of the overall story and its sequence of episodes it would be best to dispense with indications of chapter and verse. Because many readers will not be familiar with the story we will insert parenthetical references to chapter and verses to help locate episodes in the story.

the very end of the story the disciples are instructed to return to Galilee to meet the raised Jesus. As indicated in numerous references and allusions, the Galilean villagers and the residents of Jerusalem share a common Israelite cultural heritage. But the Galilean villages are places of local assemblies *(synagōgai),* family households, and people suffering a variety of sicknesses and other challenges. Life in the villages is culturally as well as geographically distant from Jerusalem and the temple, where the Passover festival is celebrated and the high priestly and Roman rulers hold sway.

Mark's characters are stereotyped, as in most ancient stories, but are those we would expect in the Galilean and Jerusalem settings.[11] Only two or three main characters appear in most episodes, along with anonymous crowds of onlookers and listeners. From the very outset, Jesus calls disciples and commissions twelve, evidently as representatives of the twelve tribes of Israel, to assist in his mission (1:16-20; 3:13-19; 6:7-13). In the village scenes, Jesus interacts with sick persons and onlookers. As the story progresses, women play an ever more prominent role (5:21-43; 7:24-30; 12:41-44; 14:3-9; 15:40-41; 15:47–16:8). "Unclean spirits" play an infrequent but significant role in the first part of the story, then disappear. Scribes and Pharisees who have come down from Jerusalem criticize and confront Jesus and early on plot to destroy him (3:1-6, 22; 7:1-5). Not until the confrontation in Jerusalem do the high priests, elders, and leading scribes, clearly the rulers based in the temple, take the lead in opposition to Jesus (11:27–12:12; 14:1-2, 43-56; 15:1). Only at the very climax of the story does Pontius Pilate appear as the Roman governor who wields power to have Jesus crucified (15:1-15). While a presence in the story, God, Jesus' "Father," and Caesar remain "offstage," as it were. While Mark's characters undergo no real psychological development of the kind typical in modern novels and films, some, particularly the disciples and women, do undergo a development in their role and relation to Jesus in the course of the story.

It is interesting to note that interpreters' rediscovery of Mark as a sustained story did not lead to immediate clarity about its plot. The

---

11. See Elizabeth Struthers Malbon, *In the Company of Jesus: Characterization in Mark's Gospel* (Louisville: Westminster John Knox, 2000), 138-56, 164-65.

dominant conflict in a story is usually the key to its plot. In traditional theological interpretation, Mark's Gospel had long been viewed in terms of individual discipleship. Some of the early readings of Mark as story tended to perpetuate this interpretation, focusing on the conflict between Jesus and his disciples that develops steadily through the story. After being called and commissioned to assist in Jesus' mission, the disciples repeatedly display their fear and misunderstanding of that mission (4:35-41; 6:47-52; 8:14-21, 27-33; 9:30-37; 10:32-40). Finally, as Jesus is arrested, tried, and crucified, the disciples abandon, betray, and deny him (14:26-50, 66-72). This reading perpetuated the modern individualistic understanding of the Gospel as a paradigmatic story of the struggle to be faithful in discipleship.

Given the several interrelated conflicts running through Mark's story, it is crucial to distinguish the dominant conflict, the key to which lies in the climax of the story. While a clear sequence of events and teachings relating to the disciples runs through Mark's narrative, the dominant conflict in the story is between Jesus and his program of preaching and healing, on the one hand, and the high priestly (and Roman) rulers and their representatives, on the other. This conflict comes to a head in the climax of the story in Jerusalem, where Jesus confronts the rulers and they respond by forming a plot to arrest him and have him killed. While the disciples' betrayal, denial, and abandonment is interwoven with the arrest, trial, and crucifixion of Jesus, Jesus' confrontation and the rulers' response drive the story.

Although the Jerusalem high priests and elders do not appear in the earlier part of the story set in Galilee — reflecting the historical fact that they had no formal jurisdiction there during Jesus' lifetime — early on the plot begins to build toward the climactic conflict in Jerusalem. That the scribes and Pharisees "come down from Jerusalem" indicates that they represent the Judean rulers. In their surveillance of Jesus they charge that he is usurping the prerogatives of the temple and priesthood by, for example, declaring the forgiveness of sin (Mark 2:1-12). After Jesus' first exorcism, the people recognize that he "teaches with authority/power," unlike the scribes (in/from Jerusalem, 1:21-28). Early in the story, the Pharisees and Herodians plot to destroy him and accuse him of working in cahoots with Satan (3:1-6, 22-28). In contrast to modern stories, there is no suspense about the outcome of these conflicts: Jesus himself announces three times that he will be arrested and condemned to death by the rulers and then will rise again (8:31; 9:30-32; 10:33-34). Framing the overall plot at the beginning and end are the conflict over who has "authority/power," Jesus or the "authorities" (1:21-28; 11:27-33), and the scribes' and later the high priests' charge of blasphemy, for which they condemn him as deserving of death (2:1-12; 14:61-64).

By comparison with the ending of the other Gospels, Mark downplays the resurrection by concluding with a scene at the empty tomb. The latter, however, forms part of the Gospel's distinctive "open" ending, in which the disciples — and the audience — are directed to go (back) to Galilee, where Jesus began his mission and where he has gone ahead after instructing them to meet him there (14:28; 16:7).

Clarity about the main plot of the story enables us to discern how Mark portrays Jesus in his interaction with the people mainly in Galilee and the Jerusalem rulers and their representatives. In numerous episodes and in several interrelated ways, Mark portrays Jesus as a prophet like Moses and Elijah, engaged in a renewal of Israel in opposition to and by the Jerusalem and Roman rulers. Preparing "the way of the Lord," and suggesting that Jesus is about to lead a new exodus, John the Baptist appears as a prophet in the wilderness, enacting a renewal of the Mosaic covenant in the dramatic ritual of a baptism of repentance (1:2-8). The baptism with Holy Spirit that Jesus will offer will further empower the new exodus and covenant — that is, the renewal of the people of Israel. That Jesus undergoes forty days' testing in the wilderness, as did Elijah in preparation for leading the renewal of Israel and Moses before leading the exodus, is another clear indication that Jesus is assuming the role of the prophet of renewal (1:12-13).

Jesus' call of the first disciples is also reminiscent of Elijah's call of Elisha and his association with the bands of prophets (Mark 1:16-20; 1 Kings 18–19). Jesus' commission of the twelve disciples is representative of the renewal (of the twelve tribes) of Israel, just as was Elijah's construction of an altar of twelve stones (Mark 3:13-19). When Jesus then goes "up the mountain" and commissions the twelve to extend his own mission of preaching and exorcism, it seems clear that he is engaged in a renewal of (the twelve tribes of) Israel (6:7-13). Similarly, the woman who had been hemorrhaging for twelve years and the almost dead twelve-year-old whom Jesus brings back to life represent the people of Israel undergoing renewal (5:21-43).

As if it were not clear enough already, the series of episodes that follows the parables speech in Mark 4 exemplifies other ways in which Jesus, as the new Moses and Elijah, is leading a renewal of Israel. This renewal is represented by two parallel sequences of five episodes each (with other episodes inserted): sea-crossing, exorcism, healings, healing, and wilderness feeding (4:35-41; 5:1-20; 5:21-43; 6:30-44; 6:47-52; 7:24-30; 7:31-37; 8:22-26). These episodes reverberate with Israelite tradition. The sea crossings suggest (again) a new exodus led by the new Moses, and the wilderness feedings are particularly suggestive of God's feeding of the people as they move along on "the way of the Lord," signaled at the outset of the story in John the Baptist's prophecy. The twelve baskets of leftovers are yet another symbol of Israel in its twelve tribes, alongside the twelve disciples and the two women who are healed. The multiplication of food also hints at Elijah's and Elisha's providing for the people, and the healings are further reminiscent of Elijah, the great prophet of renewal. Confirming Jesus in the role of new Moses and new Elijah, Mark has the founding prophet of Israel and the renewing prophet of Israel appear with Jesus on the mountain in the Transfiguration.

At the very center of Jesus' renewal of Israel, Mark's story also represents him as engaged in renewal of the Mosaic covenant, something begun by the Baptist. The Gospel portrays this explicitly at two key steps in the story: first, as Jesus, having completed his work in Galilee, heads through Judea and up to Jerusalem to confront the rulers, and then again in his words over the cup in the Passover meal just before he is arrested. In a series of dialogues Jesus delivers what is in effect a "charter" of renewed covenantal teaching to his followers (10:2-11, 13-16, 17-31, 32-45). The first dialogue refers to the commandment prohibiting adultery and the third dialogue quotes most of the covenantal commandments explicitly, and in all of them Jesus delivers law- or commandment-like statements. Closer to the climax, the words "this is my blood of the covenant, which is poured out for many" over the cup clearly allude to the basins of blood at the original covenant ceremony on Sinai (Exodus 24). Jesus thus transforms the Passover meal celebrating the exodus liberation, which he will again celebrate in the kingdom, into a covenant renewal ceremony (the term "new covenant" is in Paul, 1 Cor 11:23-26, but not in Mark 14:22-25).

Jesus' renewal of the Mosaic covenant as a central aspect of the renewal of the people is also evident in earlier episodes. In healing the paralytic he addresses the misconstrual of the covenant in self-blame for sickness in his declaration, "your sins are forgiven!" His voiding of the punishment for sins, like John's baptism of repentance, empowers the people to forgive one another and, with "a new lease on life," to pursue renewal of personal and community life (2:1-12). Immediately after the episode in which Jesus insists that in his exorcisms the rule of God has prevailed over that of "the strong man," he declares that the criterion of membership in the renewed familial community of mothers and brothers and sisters is "doing the will of God" (3:31-35). As should be well-known from the parallel lines of the first petition in the Lord's Prayer, in Israelite tradition "doing the will of God" was a synonym for covenant keeping as well as for living directly under the rule/kingdom of God.

Most dramatically in the climactic events in Jerusalem but throughout the story as well, Mark portrays Jesus carrying out his renewal of Israel in opposition to and by the Jerusalem rulers and, indirectly, also the Roman rulers. Jesus preempts the prerogatives of the temple and priesthood in healing leprosy and the forgiveness of sins (1:40-45; 2:1-12). In contrast with the scribes, he speaks and acts with authority (power) in the interests of the people (1:21-28). In response to criticism by the scribes and Pharisees, he condemns "traditions of the elders" that encourage poor peasants to devote *(korban)* some of their produce to the support of the temple, thereby preventing the people from keeping the basic covenantal commandment of God (7:1-13).

The festive entry into Jerusalem for the Passover celebration of the people's exodus liberation leads into Jesus' sustained confrontation with the high priests and their representatives in the temple courtyard. Jesus' journey to Jerusalem for the celebration of Passover suggests that his provocative actions and prophetic statements are a continuation of the new exodus in his renewal of the people. The people's cry of "Hosanna" ("Save!") was drawn from the Hallel Psalms (113-118) that the people sang at Passover, which began by recounting the exodus and entry into the land. Mark mentions repeatedly that Jesus' actions and pronouncements against the rulers, supported by the crowds, were intended as a condemnation of their rule (11:12–12:44).

Jesus' condemnation of their rule, in actions and pronouncements, are continuations of his renewal of the Mosaic covenant, which supplies the criteria for God's judgment of the temple, the high priests, and their scribal and Pharisaic representatives. The reference to Jeremiah's prophetic condemnation of the temple indicates that Jesus' demonstration in the temple is a symbolic prophetic act symbolizing condemnation by God (11:13-17). The reason announced for God's impending destruction of the temple in Jeremiah's prophecy (Jeremiah 7) was the rulers' systematic exploitation of the people in violation of the covenant commandments, only to take refuge in the temple like brigands robbing people and then seeking safety in their stronghold. Jesus' prophetic parable of the tenants draws on the traditional image of Israel as God's vineyard, in clear reference to Isaiah's well-known prophecy against the rulers for oppression of the people in violation of covenant commands (Mark 12:1-9; Isaiah 5). The application of the analogy in the parable pronounces God's imminent action against the Jerusalem rulers as tenants who have failed to care for God's vineyard, the people of Israel. A few episodes later, Jesus also condemns the scribes for "devouring widow's houses" — that is, for preying on the poor in urging them to give their scarce resources to the temple, thus leaving them without even subsistence livelihood (12:38-44). At the conclusion of the confrontation, in narrative transition to Jesus' speech on the future, Mark has him announce that the temple will be destroyed (13:1-2).

In the climax of the story, finally, Mark frames the high priests' arrest and condemnation and the Romans' crucifixion of Jesus with Jesus' continuation of his renewal of Israel. On the eve of his arrest and trial, as noted just above, Jesus transforms the Passover meal commemorating the exodus into a ceremonial renewal of Mosaic covenant, also giving instructions to the twelve to meet him back in Galilee (14:22-28). And at the empty tomb after his crucifixion, the women are given the message to meet him in Galilee, evidently to continue the renewal of Israel that he had begun.

It seems clear that virtually throughout the story, Mark portrays Jesus as engaged in the renewal of Israel in opposition to and by the rulers. Jesus' proclamations and actions, his announcement of the kingdom, his healings and exorcisms, and his conflicts with the Pharisees and confrontations with the rulers were components of that larger agenda.

The Series of Speeches in Q

Just as Mark and the other narrative Gospels are finally being taken seriously as plotted stories, the teachings of Jesus found in Matthew and Luke but not in Mark are being recognized as a series of speeches. The old fragmentation of Jesus' teachings into individual sayings determined the understanding of these teachings when they were first recognized as a common source of Matthew and Luke and classified as "the Sayings Source," "Q." This classification persisted in the move by scholars eager to claim Q as an authoritative early "Gospel" source in the recent label "Sayings Gospel," by analogy with the later Gospel of Thomas. At least some American scholars, however, are now recognizing that "Q" consisted of a series of short, traditional speeches on issues of concern to a Jesus movement.[12]

Since Q is not a story, it would be inappropriate to speak of its "plot." The first several speeches of Q, however, present what seems to be an intelligible sequence of topics.[13] First, John the Baptist announces that the coming one will baptize in Spirit and fire — renewal and judgment (Luke 3:7-9, 16-17). The first speech of Jesus, the longest and most prominent in the Q series, is a statement of covenant renewal, recognizable from its adaptation of the components of the Mosaic covenant form, beginning with the offer of the kingdom of God to the poor and hungry as the new

12. John Kloppenborg, *The Formation of Q* (Philadelphia: Fortress, 1987); Horsley, "Q and Jesus"; Alan Kirk, *The Composition of the Sayings Source* (Leiden: Brill, 1998); James M. Robinson, Paul Hoffmann, and John Kloppenborg, eds., *The Critical Edition of Q* (Minneapolis: Fortress, 2000). Ideally readers of this book would pause at this point to read the Q speeches as presented in poetic form in Richard Horsley, *Jesus in Context: Power, People, and Performance* (Minneapolis: Fortress, 2008), 229-45.

13. Following standard convention, passages in Q are cited by the corresponding chapter and verse numbers in the Gospel of Luke.

declaration of deliverance (Luke 6:20-49). Next comes Jesus' response to the Baptist's disciples, in which he declares that he is the coming one who is now fulfilling the longings of the people for healing and good news and links the Baptist and himself in the coming of the kingdom (Luke 7:18-35). Jesus then sends his envoys two-by-two to village communities to extend his own mission of preaching the kingdom and expelling demons (Luke 9:57-62; 10:2-16).

In the ensuing speeches, Jesus focuses on matters such as prayer (Luke 11:2-4, 9-13), what is happening in his exorcisms (11:14-26), woes against the scribes and Pharisees followed by pronouncement of judgment (11:39-52), how to handle being dragged into court (12:2-12), being single-minded in pursuing the kingdom of God despite desperate poverty (lack of food and shelter; 12:22-31), prophetic statements and a parable pronouncing God's condemnation of the ruling house of Jerusalem (13:28-29, 34-35), the suddenness of judgment as a sanction on all the preceding speeches (17:23-37), and a final charge to his twelve disciples to lead the deliverance of the twelve tribes (22:28-30). Most of the speeches feature "the kingdom of God" in a prominent position as the theme that unites the whole series.

The Q series of speeches thus portrays Jesus on a mission of renewal of Israel in opposition to the Jerusalem rulers and their scribal/Pharisaic representatives. As the speaker in these speeches, Jesus takes the role of a prophet. What is more, in several of the speeches he represents himself and the Baptist as the final in the long line of Israelite prophets, many of whom were killed by the rulers for their warnings. Baptizing with Spirit and fire is clearly an agenda of renewal of the people, as is Jesus' own standard list of his actions in fulfillment of longings previously articulated in prophetic oracles (e.g., Isa 35:5-6; 42:6-7; 61:1). Central in his program is the enactment in performative speech of the renewal of the covenant community (Luke 6:20-49). And the commissioning of envoys expands the program of renewal into wider circles of village communities. The petitions for sufficient food and (mutual) cancellation of debts in the prayer for the coming of the kingdom of God indicate the concretely economic implications of the renewal (11:2-4). The "punch line" of the Beelzebul speech declares that Jesus' exorcisms "by the finger of God" constitute, in effect, a new exodus (11:20). His prophetic woes against the Pharisees, rhetorically mocking their obsession with purity issues, condemn them mainly for the exploitation of people in misappropriation of their scribal role (Luke 11:39-52). And in the traditional form of a prophetic lament, Jesus pronounces a condemnation on the ruling house of Jerusalem for having killed the prophets who were sent to warn them. While the rulers stand under God's condemnation, the kingdom of God is emerging as the renewal of the people of Israel in its ideal twelve tribes.

Thus, in a series of speeches, material very different from the sequence of episodes narrated in Mark but with several overlaps of subjects/issues, Q presents a parallel portrayal of Jesus as a prophet pursuing the renewal of Israel in opposition to and by the rulers of Israel. The Gospels of Matthew and Luke both follow the Markan story, while inserting the Q speeches of Jesus at different points (the now standard hypothesis of the relationship between the three "Synoptic Gospels"). Not surprisingly, therefore, in their combination of Mark's story and the Q speeches, both Matthew and Luke also portray Jesus as engaged in the renewal of Israel in opposition to and by the rulers of Israel.

CHAPTER FOUR

Hearing the Whole Story

That we must take the Gospels "whole" as the starting point and
sources for investigation of the historical Jesus is being powerfully reinforced by recent research in text criticism and ancient communications
media. As mentioned in chapter 3 above, largely separate lines of research
in several areas are challenging standard assumptions and procedures in
study of the Gospels and Jesus. The implications of these lines of research
are only beginning to become clear. The following discussion must therefore be provisional as we struggle to discern how to move beyond assumptions that can now seen as unwarranted and to rethink the character of the
Gospels as stories and as sources for understanding Jesus.

In what has long been standard study of the Gospels, interpreters
have assumed that specialists in text criticism have established the
"best" or the "earliest" Greek text, which is readily available in standard
editions. More inquisitive scholars might occasionally check the textual
"variants" listed in the apparatus of the critical editions of the Greek text,
still trusting that we are working with something close to an original or
early text. Similarly, when we have read modern translations of the Greek
text, we have simply assumed the critical work of specialists who have
"established" the standard text from which teams of scholars have made
relatively faithful translations.

That telltale phrase "textual variants," however, is a clear indication of how interpretation of the Bible, the Sacred Scripture, is based on the assumptions and aesthetics of print-culture, with its standardized invariant text available to the eye on the printed page.[1] Indeed, established academic interpretation of the Bible is a function of the visual fixation on the biblical text *in print,* from which interpretation takes its departure. Corollary assumptions are that an "author" "wrote" each "book" which was "in circulation" and subsequently "read" by early Christians. "Judaism," followed by "Christianity," was a religion of the book, and "the Jews," followed by "the Christians," were a people of the book.

Embedded in these assumptions, therefore, professional interpreters of the Bible have been understandably slow — or reluctant — to come to grips with the implications of recent research on the communications culture of the ancient world. With the increasing specialization and "balkanization" of biblical studies, moreover, it has become difficult for specialists on the Gospels or the historical Jesus to stay abreast of research even in closely related research fields. Such research, however, is challenging some of the most basic assumptions on which previous investigation of the Gospels and Jesus has been based. It is necessary to come to grips with the implications of this research in order to understand the way the Gospels functioned as stories and how they can be used as sources for (the historical) Jesus.[2]

The Dominance of Oral Communication and the Role of Writing

Only recently have some biblical interpreters, along with some students of ancient Near Eastern and Greco-Roman civilizations, come to recog-

---

1. John Dagenais, *The Ethics of Reading in Manuscript Culture: Glossing the* Libro de buen amor (Princeton: Princeton University Press, 1994) makes interesting reading for those socialized into standard biblical studies.

2. For a somewhat fuller summary of recent research in various areas and its implication for study of the Gospels and Jesus, see Richard Horsley, "Oral Communication, Oral Performance, and New Testament Interpretation," pp. 125-56 in *Method and Meaning: Essays on New Testament Interpretation in Honor of Harold W. Attridge,* ed. Andrew B. McGowan and Kent Harold Richards (Resources for Biblical Study 67; Atlanta: Society of Biblical Literature, 2011).

nize that communications in antiquity were predominantly oral. In the initial excitement of the scholarly "discovery" that ancient societies were dominated by oral communication, a stark contrast was drawn between literacy and orality as two distinct mentalities. In retrospect, what appeared to be a "great divide" between orality and literacy turned out to be mainly between the print-culture in which Western scholarship and modern culture more generally are deeply embedded and the oral communications that dominated most historical societies. In antiquity, there would have been no sharp divide between the literate, for whom communication was still predominantly oral, and the non-literate, who knew of the existence of writing even though they could not read.

For scholars who have been simply assuming widespread literacy in antiquity, recent research that demonstrates the limited rates of literacy may come as a shock. Proficiency in reading was limited to a scribal elite in the ancient Near East and to the political-cultural elite in ancient Greece and the Roman Empire. Well-documented studies have demonstrated that in the Roman Empire what we today call "literacy" was confined to a tiny minority of the urban population, with an even smaller number in Roman Palestine and the ancient Near East possessing basic reading and writing skills.[3] Among villagers and urban artisans virtually all interaction took place orally, face to face. Even "legal" agreements such as loans were conducted orally, governed by custom and ritual. Witnesses and personal testimony were viewed as far more trustworthy than documents written by a literate elite that could be altered and used against common people.

More significant than the rate of literacy in antiquity were the social functions of writing, which was used mainly by the political and cultural elite, often as an instrument of power over the people. By the first century BCE, some wealthy Judeans, like Roman aristocratic families, had written contracts drawn up for major transactions such as large loans. The highly trained slaves in the "family of Caesar" carried out extensive correspondence in the administration of the empire. The "census" of how

3. See here especially the seminal studies of William V. Harris, *Ancient Literacy* (Cambridge: Harvard University Press, 1989), and Catherine Hezser, *Jewish Literacy in Roman Palestine* (Tübingen: Mohr Siebeck, 2001).

much tribute could be taken from the population of a given province was kept in writing (as in the "enrollment" of Luke 2:1). Extensive writing was also deployed for the operations of the Roman military. By far the principal use of writing was to facilitate the maintenance or expansion of military, economic, or social power.

Contrary to previous scholarly impressions, writing played a somewhat limited role in elite "literary" culture that, like other aspects of life in antiquity, was largely oral. Poetry of various forms was performed at festivals and plays in theaters. Orators declaimed at city festivals and proclaimed the virtues and benefactions of emperors at the imperial court. Some used writing to prepare for their oral performances. At least some literary culture was requisite for the urban and provincial elite of the Roman Empire. Yet even for the imperial, provincial, and urban elite, most of life, including the ceremonial conduct of "political" affairs and "literary" entertainment, proceeded in one or another form of oral communication. Even the written texts used by the literate elite were ancillary to the predominant oral communication.

In coming to grips with the relationship between writing and oral communication in antiquity, it is also necessary to consider the various kinds of writing and people's attitudes toward and relations to them. In modern print culture it is simply assumed that writing is for reading. Accordingly, in biblical studies it is usually assumed that "biblical" texts were read and interpreted. But there were different kinds of writing in traditional societies, and some written texts were not produced to be read or later consulted, much less studied.[4]

Virtually any writing in a society dominated by oral communication appeared to have a certain numinous quality that lent it a seemingly transcendent authority. The books of the Pentateuch later included in the Hebrew Bible provide a most vivid example in the writing of God, "the finger of YHWH" engraving commandments on stone in the theophany at Sinai (Exod 24:12; 31:18; 32:16; Deut 4:13; 5:22; 9:10). When the stone tablets were then placed in the ark of the covenant, the ark also became charged with

---

4. See especially Susan Niditch, *Oral World and Written Word: Ancient Israelite Literature* (Louisville: Westminster John Knox, 1996); on second temple texts see Richard Horsley, *Scribes, Visionaries, and the Politics of Second Temple Judea* (Louisville: Westminster John Knox, 2007), chapters 5 and 6.

divine power. But the writing was not for communication, which happened rather when Moses recited "the words" of God orally "into the ears of" the people. The function of the numinous aura of the divine writing was to lend the "words" awesome power and authority.

In largely non-literate societies, this "monumental" function of written texts tends to enhance the prestige of their presumed contents even when most people cannot read them. Prominent in the cities of the Roman Empire, for example, were monumental arches inscribed with the great acts of the emperors, important in the legitimation of imperial power relations. An important study of the Domesday Book of medieval England concludes that this text was not a record to be consulted or read but an awe-inspiring symbol of the grand, unalterable Norman conquest by William the Conqueror.[5] Overlapping in function was what we might call "constitutional" writing that helped authorize or legitimize political-economic-religious institutions and structures. This is illustrated by the inscription of laws on public monuments in the Greek city-states, not to communicate the content of the laws to (largely non-literate) people, but rather to produce a public display of their force and permanence.

In second temple Judea what corresponded to the writing of laws on stone in Greek city-states was the writing of the Torah (or covenant or laws of Moses) on large parchment scrolls. Such numinous (monumental and) constitutional writings were not primarily for reading or consultation. References to such writings in the books of the Pentateuch later included in the Hebrew Bible indicate how at least scribal circles understood these "writings of the Torah." After God's initial numinous writing of the covenant "words" on stone and after Moses placed a numinous writing in the ark (Deut 31:24-26; cf. 28:58-61), Joshua "wrote the teaching *(torah)* of Moses on the stones [of the altar he had built]," making the numinous constitutional writing ("literally") visible on stone monuments (Josh 8:30-35; cf. 24:25-27). Again, communication of the words to the people was oral, in Joshua's recitation. The monumental writing of the covenantal teaching served to externalize and eternalize the covenant between Yahweh and Israel, "underwriting" its continuing force.

5. M. T. Clanchy, *From Memory to Written Record: England, 1066-1307* (Cambridge: Harvard University Press, 1979), 18.

Surely the clearest illustration of the fact that the "books" of Torah were produced, not for widespread reading and consultation, but rather as numinous monuments is the ceremonial public presentations of the "writing of the teaching" by the learned scribe Ezra (Nehemiah 8). Standing on a raised wooden platform, Ezra "opened the writing (presumably a large scroll) in the sight of all the people." The people then exclaimed "'Amen, Amen,' lifting up their hands," and "bowed their heads and worshipped Yahweh with their faces to the ground." This "writing of the teaching of Moses" was clearly a sacred object of great power. The people were bowing before a numinous monumental writing.

Such numinous, monumental writing served to authorize or legitimate or "constitute" the ruling institutions of Israel, the temple-state and high priesthood. Like many writings placed in temples in Egypt and Mesopotamia, written scrolls of Mosaic Torah were laid up in the Jerusalem temple, further enhancing their authority, and were not intended primarily for reading or consultation, although learned scribes probably had their contents "written on the tablets of their hearts," as we shall see.

Villagers, Scribes, and Scrolls

Yet other, largely separate lines of recent research are showing that even learned scribes who copied and preserved written texts nevertheless cultivated texts orally. We should not imagine that scribal culture was exclusively written, since scribes' knowledge of texts was what might be called "oral-written." Nor should we imagine that popular culture was exclusively oral, since villagers knew of the existence of written texts. But while learned scribes highly valued the written texts that they worked with, ordinary people were ambivalent about written texts, viewing what stood written as holding a special authority, on the one hand, yet as belonging to the elite, on the other.

It has long been known that the Pharisees, while they presumably knew and revered the laws of Moses that were written on scrolls, also cultivated orally "the ancestral traditions," regulations that (depending on the favor of the current high priest) were included in the laws of the temple-state (that is, held authority as official tradition). Recent research into scribal practices in the ancient Near Eastern regimes and Judah/ Judea is now showing that the Pharisees were hardly unique among learned scribes. Learning to read and write was integral to the training of professional scribes, and inscribing texts on scrolls was an important activity in their service to temple-states and imperial regimes. Professional scribes in the service of kings and temples, however, learned and cultivated texts orally, by repeated recitation.[6] In Judea, the purpose of scribal training was the formation of character suited for service to the temple-state. The skills of reading and writing were fundamental, yet ancillary to the inculcation of personal discipline and obedience to authority.

Scribal training, while it included writing and reading, proceeded mainly in an oral-aural mode. In the early second century BCE the learned scribe Jesus Ben Sira declared that in his "house of instruction" he taught not by asking his students to "open a book" but by "opening his mouth" (Sir 51:23-25). His teaching was oral, and his students' reception was aural. The curriculum included Torah and prophecies as well as various kinds of wisdom (39:1-3). Scribes learned all such texts by repeated recitation, so that the texts became "written on the tablet of the heart" (Prov 3:3), a metaphor that points to the essential role and importance of memory in the cultivation of texts. As in elite medieval European culture, manuscripts were produced but were simply reference points for the oral-aural-memorial cycle of repeated recitation by which texts continued their life.

This oral-performative scribal tradition was central in the Qumran community, which also produced and valued written scrolls. In contrast to standard translations that project modern scholars' own practices of "reading," "studying," and "interpreting" written texts into antiquity, a more appropriate translation of a now famous passage in the Community Rule would be:

6. David M. Carr, *Writing on the Tablet of the Heart* (Oxford: Oxford University Press, 2005), summarizes recent research on scribal practice in ancient Egyptian and Mesopotamian regimes and discusses the similar practice among the scribes in the monarchy of Judah and the Judean temple-state. Horsley, *Scribes, Visionaries,* especially chapters 5-7, discusses scribal practice in the Judean temple-state. Martin S. Jaffee, *Torah in the Mouth* (Oxford: Oxford University Press, 2001), presents an illuminating examination of scribal practice in the Qumran community and especially among successive generations of rabbinic circles.

> Where the ten are . . . the many shall watch in community for a
> third of every night of the year, to recite the writing [*lqrw' bspr*]
> and to search the justice-ruling [*ldrws mspt*] and to offer commu-
> nal blessings [*lbrk byhd*]. (1QS 6.6-8)

All three of the activities mentioned here — recitation, "searching," and
uttering blessings — were clearly oral. The "writing" mentioned is usually assumed to have been a "book" of "the Torah." But even if a scroll of
Torah were open before the reciter(s), recitation would have been largely
from memory. Torah was recited at Qumran, moreover, just as texts were
learned by scribes in training by recitation, not for external study and interpretation but to internalize spiritual and moral discipline, in this case
collective as well as individual. The result was also the oral-memorial
knowledge of texts that had become "written on the tablets of the heart,"
many of which were also written on scrolls possessed by the scribal-
priestly community at Qumran and/or laid up in the temple. Whether or
not they consulted scrolls on a regular basis, learned (literate) scribes in
Judea evidently knew the contents of what had become authoritative
written texts by having recited them orally and held them in their memory to be recited and applied as appropriate to situations in the life of the
temple-state.

The importance of oral cultivation of authoritative texts by learned
scribes helps explain and is confirmed by yet another largely independent line of recent research, the intensive text-critical examination of
the multiple scrolls of texts that were later included in the Hebrew Bible
found among the Dead Sea Scrolls. Text critics of these recently discovered manuscripts are drawing two related fundamental conclusions
about the texts of the books of the Pentateuch and prophets: multiple
"versions" of these books coexisted, and the two or sometimes three dis-
tinguishable textual traditions were all still developing.[7] In the emerging
critical perspective on the origins and development of these texts, it is
evident that they were multiform in late second temple times, their
wording not yet standardized. As scribes cultivated the authoritative

---

7. See Eugene Ulrich, *The Dead Sea Scrolls and the Origins of the Bible* (Grand
Rapids: Eerdmans, 1999).

texts and made new copies, they continued to enrich them, adding to them and/or adapting them. There appears to have been a dynamic relationship between the oral cultivation (learning and recitation) of these texts and the production of additional manuscripts (scrolls).

If literate scribes cultivated texts, along with the broader cultural tradition, orally, how much more did the non-literate ordinary people cultivate their own popular cultural tradition orally?[8] While they probably had little direct knowledge of written authoritative Judean texts, Galilean, Samaritan, and Judean villagers were thoroughly familiar with Israelite traditions, including stories of prophets like Moses, Joshua, and Elijah and of the popular acclamation of the young David as messiah. As noted in chapter 1, these stories remained vividly alive among villagers in Jesus' time, so much so that they determined the social forms of popular prophetic and messianic movements.[9] In another telling illustration of the operation of popular Israelite tradition, Josephus's accounts of Galileans who attacked Antipas's palace in Tiberias or Herodian officials elsewhere indicate that the people were acting in defense of Mosaic covenantal commandments that had long been the traditional basis of social-economic life among the villages.[10] As in other agrarian societies, the popular tradition paralleled but differed in emphases and implication from the official or "great" tradition, which was enshrined in written form as well as cultivated orally by the scribes.[11] The cultural context in which Jesus worked and in which the Gospel tradition developed would thus have been the Israelite popular tradition that continued to be cultivated orally in village communities. This tradition over-

8. Fuller discussion in Richard Horsley with Jonathan A. Draper, *Whoever Hears You Hears Me: Prophets, Performance and Tradition in Q* (Harrisburg: Trinity, 1999), especially chapters 5 and 6.

9. See further Richard Horsley with John S. Hanson, *Bandits, Prophets, and Messiahs: Popular Resistance Movements at the Time of Jesus* (Minneapolis: Winston, 1985), chapters 3 and 4.

10. For references and analysis see Richard Horsley, *Galilee: History, Politics, People* (Harrisburg: Trinity, 1995), 152-55.

11. Especially helpful is James C. Scott, "Protest and Profanation: Agrarian Revolt and the Little Tradition," *Theory and Society* 4 (1977), 1-38, 211-46. For application to Jesus and the Gospels, see the essays in Richard Horsley, ed., *Hidden Transcripts and the Arts of Resistance* (Semeia Studies 48; Atlanta: Society of Biblical Literature, 2004).

lapped with, but had significant differences of emphasis from, the official tradition that was partly enshrined in written texts (as noted in chapter 1).

The more extensive recent studies of orality and writing in Roman Palestine have found that, corresponding to the way writing was often used as an instrument of power, ordinary Galileans and Judeans, like non-literate people in other societies, were ambivalent in their attitude toward writing. People were understandably resentful at the use of written records that they could not read but that might be used against them, for example, to take control of their land. One of the first actions in the popular insurrection in Jerusalem in 66 CE was to "destroy the money-lenders' bonds and prevent the recovery of debts" (Josephus, *War* 2.426-27).

The ordinary people's attitudes toward the "Scriptures" was more ambivalent. While villagers and even ordinary Jerusalemites probably did not have much direct contact with scrolls of Scripture, they certainly knew of their existence and knew that the rulers and their retainers claimed them as authoritative texts. Insofar as these written texts possessed a numinous aura, the monumental and constitutional scrolls of Torah and Prophets laid up in the temple held a certain awesome authority of permanence for the Judean villagers, and perhaps even Samaritan and Galilean villagers as well. It seems highly likely that Judean villagers would have known and revered the sacred scrolls as having a special authority just because they were "written." This reverence is illustrated by Josephus's account of an incident in which a widespread protest was sparked when a Roman soldier on a search and destroy mission tore up a scroll of "the sacred law" in a village near Jerusalem (*War* 2.228-30; *Antiquities* 20.114-16).

Yet despite its special authority of standing "written" on sacred scrolls, the common people seem to have held a somewhat ambivalent attitude toward "the Scripture" or "the Law" and its scribal brokers. This ambivalence is reflected in the Gospels. The terms "Scripture" and "it is written" (*graphē* and *gegraptai* respectively) have usually been understood as "quotation formulas," especially since a few words ostensibly cited from a written text often follow. But these terms are more likely references to the authoritative "Scripture" generally. They are references to the authority of passages that stand "written" more than signals that certain passages are being "quoted."[12] Even for scribes, "quotations" would have been from memory, not from a written scroll.

In the Gospel of Mark, not only do *gegraptai* ("it has been written") and *graphē* ("writing") signal the authority of what stands written in official texts, but most such references are aimed polemically against the official cultivators of these texts. For example, Jesus cites Isaiah against the scribes and Pharisees in Mark 7:6 and later cites Jeremiah and a festival psalm against the rulers of the temple (11:17; 12:10), each time intensifying his criticism with the phrase "it is written." In Mark 9:12-13 Jesus appeals to the general authority of Scripture (no particular reference is given) against the scribal authorities on Scripture. Knowing that certain references that stand "written" are specially authoritative to the officials, Mark's Jesus claims that very authority against them.[13]

The Gospel of John displays even more ambivalence about or distancing of "the Scripture" or "the Law" (or "Moses"). The Law is "theirs," it belongs to "the Judeans," that is, to the high priests and the Pharisees, to whom Moses gave it (John 10:34-35; 15:25; 7:19). Indeed, the Judean rulers could appeal to the Law of Moses as their authority in conflict with Jesus and judge him according to "their law" (7:19, 22-23; 10:34-35; 15:25; 18:34; 19:7). Yet since they do not keep it, Moses ironically testifies against them (7:19). On the other hand, insofar as the "Scripture/Law" was authoritative for the rulers of "the Judeans" with whom Jesus and the Johannine movement were in conflict, John could also appeal to it as authoritative in claims about Jesus. "Moses wrote about" Jesus, and Jesus was the fulfillment of "their Law/Scripture" (1:45; 5:45-46; 13:18; 15:25; 19:24, 28, 36, 37, etc.). This high regard among ordinary people for what stood written as authoritative and permanent may well be what led to the writing down of John's story itself, so that it would be all the more effective in leading hearers/"readers" to "trust that Jesus is the Messiah" (20:30-31).[14]

12. See Ian Henderson, "*Didache* and Orality in Synoptic Comparison," *Journal of Biblical Literature* 111 (1992), 292.

13. For further discussion, see Richard Horsley, *Hearing the Whole Story: The Politics of Plot in Mark's Gospel* (Louisville: Westminster John Knox, 2001), 59-61, 156-76.

14. For further discussion, see Tom Thatcher, *Why John Wrote a Gospel: Jesus-Memory-History* (Louisville: Westminster John Knox, 2006).

Composition and Continuing Performance

In the context of modern print-culture we have imagined the Gospels to be "written" by "authors," such as "Matthew," "Mark," and "John," and then, perhaps after some "editing," being "read." But given the predominance of oral communication and the lack of literacy among ordinary people, it now appears that the Gospels, which are popular stories about a popular leader and his movement, were composed in an ongoing process of repeated performance of the Gospel stories in community gatherings.

The genesis of the Gospels is evident in the numerous features of oral discourse in the narratives and speeches. So far, exploration of these features has focused primarily on the Gospel of Mark and the parallel speeches in Matthew and Luke, commonly referred to as "Q." These oral features are perhaps most readily evident in the Q speeches, as becomes particularly clear once we discern that these speeches are poetry.[15] In the Greek text, the Q discourses clearly consist of sequences of parallel lines, with frequent repetition of words, parallel verb forms, and word endings (= sounds/morphemes) and connections of terms, sounds, and themes across the several lines of a speech. Extensive work has also been done on oral patterns in Mark, including the repetition of themes and kinds of episodes, the framing of some episodes by others, repeated triplet patterns within and across episodes, and the interweaving of subplots.[16]

Only recently has exploration of the possible oral composition of the

15. See here Horsley with Draper, *Whoever Hears You Hears Me,* where a number of key Q speeches are printed in ways that visually emphasize parallel lines and repetition of sounds.

16. See especially the analysis of Mark's healing, exorcism, and parable episodes in the pioneering work of Werner Kelber, *The Oral and Written Gospel* (Philadelphia: Fortress, 1983); the collected essays of Pieter Botha, *Orality and Literacy in Early Christianity* (Eugene: Cascade, 2012); and the collected articles of Joanna Dewey on the oral features of Mark's narrative in *Orality, Scribality, and the Gospel of Mark* (Eugene: Cascade, 2013). See also the essays by Thatcher, Thatcher and Kelber, Horsley, Dewey, and Kelber in Tom Thatcher, ed., *Jesus, the Voice, and the Text: Beyond the Oral and Written Gospel* (Waco: Baylor University Press, 2008); and the well-crafted explanation of why and how Mark must be understood as composed in performance in Antoinette Clark Wire, *The Case for Mark Composed in Performance* (Eugene: Cascade, 2011).

Gospel of John begun.[17] Recent studies emphasize key oral features in the narrative, such as repetition of sounds and words, figurative language, the presence of traditional speech genres like the riddle, use of direct discourse, scenes with only two characters, and the structure of audience address, all of which are traces of a process of composition in successive oral performances. Much of the Fourth Gospel consists of short parallel or supplementary clauses that make for effective immediate communication between performer and hearers. John's narrator is a skillful storyteller, proceeding slowly, step by step, building with symbolic terms and allusions that resonate with those embedded in Israelite popular tradition and are suspicious of the official Jerusalem institutions and tradition. In the complex episodes that move from Jesus' performance of a sign to dialogue with Judeans and/or to monologue by Jesus, one can sense John working the audience toward punch-line declarations: "I AM the Living Bread/Light/Resurrection and Life/True Vine." The developing story circles around, builds tension and symbolism, and drives home the point.

Lest it be difficult for us to recognize that stories from among the people could be composed in a process of oral communication — that is, without an "author" having composed it in writing (as we moderns compose) — it is now clear that even the literate elite in the Roman Empire did not compose their letters or histories or other texts in writing. To take an example familiar to students of early Christianity, Pliny the Younger — famous for his letters to Emperor Trajan that discuss the proper way to deal with Christians — offers a fascinating account of his own literary practice (*Letters* 2.10; 3.18; 7.17; 9.34).[18] Awaking before daylight, Pliny composed in his head while lying in bed. Rising after some hours, he called in a capable secretary to take dictation as he spoke his text. To disseminate his compositions he performed them (read/recited) them orally to groups of friends or in public. Pliny's "public-ation" of his com-

17. See now the collection of essays in Anthony Le Donne and Tom Thatcher, eds., *The Fourth Gospel in First Century Media Culture* (London: Continuum, 2011), especially the essays by Thatcher, Boomershine, Wire, and Dunn.

18. For discussion of Pliny and wider compositional practices in antiquity see Jocelyn Penny Small, *Wax Tablets of the Mind: Cognitive Studies of Memory and Literacy in Classical Antiquity* (New York: Routledge, 1997).

positions was thus assisted or backed up by a written text, but his compositional method in no way resembled the processes through which the book you are now reading was produced.

Many texts in antiquity were "traditional" in the sense that they were repeatedly recited or performed orally. The best-known examples are surely the *Iliad* and the *Odyssey*. While it remains convenient to refer to "Homer" as the "author" of these works, classics scholars are now well aware that the name "Homer" is a cipher, a personification of an entire performance tradition, and that these poetic epics not only were never composed in writing but that their texts developed over centuries of re-peated performance. Of course, in the case of the Gospels, which are much shorter than the Homeric epics, the span of time between the de-velopment of the story and its commitment to written form took place within decades, not centuries. The existence of fragmentary papyri of Gospel texts (the Gospel of John specifically) from the early second cen-tury indicates that the writing of the gospel story happened fairly early. It is not difficult to imagine that at least one possible motive for a commu-nity of Christ or its leader(s) to produce a written version of their Jesus stories was to give the story the greater authority of standing written. The ending of John's Gospel suggests just such a motive: "these things are writ-ten that you may come to trust," for "we know that [this] witness is true" (John 20:30-31; 21:24). Throughout John's story, Jesus does signs and makes arguments so that Galileans or Samaritans or Judeans will come to trust in him. That these things were later "written" made all those signs and discourses all the more authoritative, so that the hearers of the Gos-pel would be persuaded to trust in Jesus as the Messiah (or Light or Life).

Not only were the Gospels produced through oral-memorial pro-cesses, they also continued to be performed orally in communities of Christ long after they were written, alongside other authoritative stories and sayings of Jesus that had not been written down. While biblical scholars have been sensitive to this fact since the rise of form criticism in the early-twentieth century, it was in fact standard practice in Greco-Roman antiquity generally. Ancient "literature" was typically experi-enced through recitations or performances before groups, not through mass distribution of physical manuscripts or through silent reading alone and in private — in other words, not in the way that readers today experience texts. Greek and Latin dramas were performed publicly in elaborately staged productions. Poetry and odes were chanted or sung. Even histories were "published" by performance before groups of listeners, ranging from private gatherings in the homes of the wealthy to open readings at public festivals. A very fluid relationship existed between composition, performance, and written documents. Like the Judean scribes, performers became thoroughly familiar with texts to be recited and often recited even lengthy compositions from memory. The existence of texts in writing did not disrupt the continuity of oral performance and certainly did not displace it.

The few pertinent early references to oral and/or written communication indicate that the communities of Christ and their nascent intellectual leadership did not just prefer orality, but were even reticent about or suspicious of writing.[19] For example, in the early second century, Papias, bishop of Hierapolis declared,

> I inquired about *the words* of the ancients, what Andrew or Peter or Philip or Thomas or James or John or Matthew or any other of the Lord's disciples *said,* and what Aristion and the elder John, the Lord's disciples, were *saying.* For I did not suppose that things from books *(ek tōn bibliōn)* would benefit me so much as *things from a living and abiding voice (zōēs phōnēs kai menousēs).* (cited by Eusebius, *Church History* 3.39.3-4)

Papias's statement illustrates both the oral mode of communication and the high value placed on the direct continuity of oral communication from the Lord through the previous two generations of disciples.

A growing number of studies, particularly of Mark and Q, are exploring how these Gospel texts would have "worked" in oral performance by drawing on interdisciplinary research into oral performance.[20] Other

---

19. Paul J. Achtemeier, "*Omne verbum sonat:* The New Testament and the Oral Environment of Late Western Antiquity," *Journal of Biblical Literature* 109 (1990), 3-27; Botha, *Orality and Literacy,* chapters 2 and 3; Whitney Shiner, *Proclaiming the Gospel: First Century Performances of Mark* (Harrisburg: Trinity, 2003).

20. For example, the essays in Dewey, *Orality . . . and Mark;* Horsley with Draper, *Whoever Hears You Hears Me;* Wire, *The Case for Mark.*

studies have shown how performance of Mark may have "worked" by comparison with known performance practices in Greek and Latin sources.[21] A *lector* of the Gospels did not need to read from a codex, but could simply learn gospel stories by hearing oral performances by others. Justin Martyr reports that at Sunday assemblies "the memoirs of the apostles or the writings of the prophets are read (= recited) for as long as time permits."[22] Hippolytus says that Scripture was "read" (recited aloud) at the beginning of the service by a succession of "readers" (reciters) until all had gathered. This practice lasted at least to the time of Augustine, who observed that many people in his day had learned to recite (large portions of) the Gospels themselves from hearing them recited in services.[23]

Ironically perhaps, for most of us socialized into a field deeply rooted in print culture, the most decisive evidence that the Gospel sources were not read from manuscripts but were communicated in continuing oral performance may be coming from the text critics, on whom we previously depended to "establish" the written text. Leading text critics of the New Testament are now drawing conclusions similar to those drawn by scholars who focus on the Qumran manuscripts of books later included in the Hebrew Bible: the earliest manuscripts are so varied that it may not be possible to establish a stable "early" written text of the Gospels.[24] Early papyri reflect several different "types" of texts, while still other early papyri show texts different from any of those types. Some "variations" in the manuscripts appear to be typical of oral-memorial compositions, with scribes acting more in the role of remembrancers and performers than mere copyists, recreating the texts with a view to

---

21. See now Shiner, *Proclaiming the Gospel,* on which the following discussion depends.

22. Shiner, *Proclaiming the Gospel,* 26, 47.

23. See further Shiner, *Proclaiming the Gospel,* 45, 107.

24. The following is based on observations by Eldon J. Epp, "The Significance of the Papyri for Determining the Nature of the New Testament Text in the Second Century: A Dynamic View of Textual Transmission," in *Gospel Traditions in the Second Century: Origins, Recensions, Text, and Transmission,* ed. William L. Petersen (Notre Dame: Notre Dame University Press, 1990), 84-103; David C. Parker, *Codex Bezae: An Early Christian Manuscript and Its Text* (Cambridge: Cambridge University Press, 1992), 24-30, 247-48, 257; Wire, *The Case for Mark,* 33-35.

the needs and concerns of their own communities. Some "copies" were evidently made not letter by letter or syllable by syllable but phrase by phrase, with variations still producing something intelligible and, in some cases, perhaps better communicating the meaning of the text. Perhaps not surprisingly, some variations appear to be typical of vernacular or "homespun" Greek.

Leading text critics are thus now finding that the early manuscripts of the Gospels exhibit the kinds of variations one would typically expect between multiple oral performances of a traditional story, sometimes with as much disagreement between the manuscripts of a single Gospel (comparing multiple manuscripts of Mark) as between different Gospels (comparing Mark and Luke).[25] Put another way, and judging from the remarkable diversity of the early manuscript tradition, the "original" text of the Gospels was *multiform*.[26] Although their own research has been quite independent of research on oral performance, text critics such as David Parker are suggesting that oral cultivation of the texts influenced and was reflected in the copying of the texts — in other words, that the early manuscripts were themselves heavily influenced by continuing oral recitation of the basic text.[27] Text critics are thus now suggesting, in ef-

---

25. Kim Haines-Eitzen, *Guardians of Letters: Literacy, Power, and the Transmission of Early Christian Literature* (Oxford: Oxford University Press, 2000), 106-7. The implications of these recent text-critical findings are devastating for interpretations of the historical Jesus that assume that the "earlier" Gospels are necessarily better sources for Jesus' individual sayings. In the context of the present study, for example, it has long been a commonplace to assume that Mark and Q are "more likely historical" than John simply because John was, by any count, written several decades later. Yet even if this is the case, the version of any particular saying that appears in a "critical edition" of Mark may actually be a product of text-critical reconstructions based on third-century manuscripts that actually show important variations. Thus, even if Mark wrote before John, the currently available text of any given saying or story in Mark may be much more recent than the available text of a passage from the Fourth Gospel. Simply put, the notion that "older is better" has been significantly problematized by recent research.

26. Eldon J. Epp, "The Multivalence of the Term 'Original Text' in New Testament Criticism," *Harvard Theological Review* 92 (1999), 245-81; "The Oxyrhynchus New Testament Papyri: 'Not without Honor Except in Their Own Hometown'?" *Journal of Biblical Literature* 123 (2004), 5-55.

27. As a mark of how independent text-critical research has been from research in closely related areas such as the oral performance of texts and social memory, Alan

fect, the even the written Gospel manuscripts were products of the repeated performance of their contents over many generations.

The Gospels in Performance as Historical Sources

The implications of recent research on ancient communications media thus put interpreters of the Gospels and Jesus in an awkward position. The text of the Gospels that we have been trained to interpret is a synthetic product of modern Western biblical studies, "established" by text critics on the basis of relatively late and complete manuscripts. Given the dominance of oral communication in the ancient world, the Gospel texts, even once they were written, functioned and lived as texts-in-performance in communities of Christ in particular life-circumstances.

As noted in chapter 3, established interpretation of Gospel texts, in which we have been trained, focuses on the meaning of words, phrases, individual sayings (verses), and discrete "pericopes" (often "lessons" for a given week in the lectionary). Text critics are now concluding that the wording of phrases, sayings, and episodes in the Gospels was unstable — until a degree of stabilization was established in late antiquity. Study of epics and other texts-in-performance in other fields, however, are finding that while the wording of lines and "stanzas" or episodes changes from performance to performance, depending on the audience and circumstances, the overall story tends to be consistent. These findings thus reinforce the recognition, discussed in the previous chapter, that the Gospels are not mere collections of sayings and miracle and pronouncement stories strung end to end, but are sustained stories (with speeches) with a dominant plot and subordinate plots.

Kirk, "Manuscript Tradition as Tertium Quid: Orality and Memory in Scribal Practice," in Thatcher, ed., *Jesus, the Voice and the Text*, 229-34, discusses the irony of how text critics such as Parker and especially Bart Ehrman continue to project print-cultural assumptions onto the manuscript tradition. Ehrman, *The Orthodox Corruption of Scripture: The Effect of Early Christological Controversies on the Text of the New Testament* (Oxford: Oxford University Press, 1993), e.g. 31, 59, 275, even accuses the scribes, whom he views as mere copyists, of "misquoting" and "tampering with" some supposedly pristine text.

The implication for the Gospels as historical sources for Jesus is clear: *the Gospels as whole stories (with speeches) are more reliable as early sources than are particular sayings or episodes, on which previous study has focused.* The implication of the study of texts-in-performance in other fields is thus powerfully reinforcing the realization in study of the Gospels that, in view of their literary integrity as stories, they must be read as whole, sustained stories. If in their own historical context they were performed stories, moreover, it would be most appropriate to *hear* the whole stories in context.

While traditional training in biblical studies has left us ill-prepared to understand the Gospels as texts-in-performance, recent studies in other fields offer assistance. Proliferating studies of one or many aspects of texts-in-performance in fields such as ancient Greek and medieval European epic, socio-linguistics, and ethnography of performance are readily available. Some of the recent experiments by biblical scholars to appreciate texts-in-performance have drawn particularly on the work of John Miles Foley, coupled with research on social-cultural memory.[28] In order to keep the presentation and procedure somewhat manageable here we focus on three key aspects of texts-in-performance derived mainly from the theoretical reflections of Foley and closely related work on social memory.

Texts-in-performance involve several "extratextual" factors as well as the "text" itself: A *text* is performed before *hearers* (audience) who interact with the performer-and-text in their life-circumstances or *context;* the community of hearers are affected by or *resonate* with the performed text as it *references* the cultural *tradition* or social memory in which both performer (and text) and hearers are rooted (the referencing is usually

---

28. John Miles Foley, *Immanent Art: From Structure to Meaning in Traditional Oral Epic* (Bloomington: Indiana University Press, 1991); *The Singer of Tales in Performance* (Bloomington: Indiana University Press, 1995); *How to Read an Oral Poem* (Urbana and Chicago: University of Illinois Press, 2002); Horsley with Draper, *Whoever Hears You Hears Me;* Alan Kirk and Tom Thatcher, eds., *Memory, Tradition, and Text: Uses of the Past in Early Christianity* (Semeia Studies 52; Atlanta: Society of Biblical Literature, 2005); Richard Horsley, et al., eds., *Performing the Gospel: Orality, Memory, and Mark* (Minneapolis: Fortress, 2006); Horsley, *Jesus in Context: Power, People, and Performance* (Minneapolis: Fortress, 2008), chapters 3-7.

"metonymic," that is, a part signals the whole). To appreciate the Gospels as texts-in-performance, therefore, we focus on the *text* as performed in *context* as it references the cultural *tradition* (memory).

Attempting to hear the *text* of each Gospel leads to taking the whole story into account, leading in turn to an appreciation of its complexity — virtually the opposite of focusing on text-fragments taken out of context one at a time, often selected according to modern theological concerns. Earlier episodes (including shorter or longer speeches) set up later episodes, which in turn shed new light on the earlier ones. Jesus is always interacting with people in specific circumstances, whether people who become his followers, those he opposes, or those who oppose him. His interactions with the common people have implications for his conflicts with the rulers and their representatives, and vice versa. The story is filled with conflict, often multiple conflicts. Jesus' actions and speeches involve multiple interests and issues simultaneously. Chapters 3 above and 5 below are our attempts to read/hear the Gospel texts as stories of interaction and conflict.

Attempting to hear the text of each Gospel *in context* requires Gospel interpreters to become as knowledgeable as possible in ancient history, particularly the history of Palestine under Roman rule and of the other areas of the Roman Empire into which Jesus movements moved in the first few generations. This history is best understood in a multidisciplinary way that accounts for concerns relating to archaeology, politics, economy, and anthropology. That the Gospels portray such sharp conflict between Jesus and the people, on the one side, and the Roman rulers and their clients, on the other, requires investigation into the political-economic-religious structures and dynamics of life in Galilee and Judea under Roman rule and other areas in which a Gospel story resonated with people. Chapters 1 and 2 in this volume represent an attempt to take seriously the historical context from which the Gospels emerged and in which their stories were first heard.

Attempting to sense how each Gospel text performed in context may have resonated with people as it referenced (predominantly Israelite) cultural *tradition* (social memory) requires Gospel interpreters to become as knowledgeable as possible in Israelite culture. This includes the differences between popular and official tradition, with attention to the ways that Galileans, Judeans, and Samaritans were impacted by outside forces, both material and cultural. In this connection, the ground is shifting under our feet as we recognize, for example, that the books of the Hebrew Bible are not necessarily direct sources for Israelite popular tradition, representing as they do the interests of the scribal class that produced them, and that the Hellenistic philosophical texts do not provide direct sources for popular culture in Hellenistic cities, much less the surrounding villages. Sections of the chapters above and below include discussion of popular and official Israelite tradition and aspects of ancient media culture that were factors in the reading/hearing of the Gospel texts.

As we shift from focusing on text-fragments as objects of interpretation to appreciation of texts-in-performance in historical and cultural context, our goal also changes. Instead of trying to establish the meaning of the text(fragment)-in-itself, we are attempting to recognize and appreciate the *work* that a performed text does in and on the community of hearers in their particular historical situation. What we are after is the effect of the performed text on the community addressed, as detected from the text in what is known of the context, including from other sources.

Recognition that our principal sources for Jesus are the Gospel texts-in-performance might appear to make historical investigation and historical knowledge virtually impossible. But that would be true only on the standard old assumptions of biblical studies and the distinctively modern Western individualistic belief that a historical person, and the revealer Jesus in particular, can be known apart from how he was embedded in societal forms and social interaction in political-economic-religious context. That an individual person and what he "actually" said and did could be isolated was a chimera of the modern Western post-Enlightenment individualistic imagination. It could be argued that what has led to the recent revival of interest in the historical Jesus has been the greater awareness and more precise knowledge of the historical situation in which he lived and worked. What has hardly begun is work on viewing and exploring Jesus relationally as well as contextually engaged in societal forms and interaction as portrayed by the Gospel stories and speeches. Recognition that our principal sources for Jesus were texts-in-performance only forces us to move toward a relational and contextual approach.

Since the Gospels were produced by and performed in communities of Jesus movements that responded to Jesus' mission, however, we not only cannot extract Jesus as an individual from his interaction with others in historical context, but we cannot extract Jesus-in-interaction from the movements that produced and performed the Gospels. This, of course, is the way history works anyhow, as a historically significant figure emerges from interrelationship and interaction with people in complex circumstances in the movements or events thus catalyzed. In attempting to appreciate how a Gospel story of Jesus' mission resonated with the community/movement in which it was performed we can discern how he was understood as interacting with his followers and his opponents in historical context in one of the key movements resulting from his mission. We could then make judicious, informed comparisons of those portrayals to ascertain what may have been the main agenda of Jesus' mission in historical context. Because of the very character of the Gospels as the sources (whole stories in performance), however, it is necessary for investigation of Jesus in historical context to begin with the broad portrayal of Jesus' mission in particular Gospels.

However, having just sketched how we might appropriately appreciate and appropriate the Gospel texts as stories or speeches in performance by attempting to hear them in context, we must also acknowledge that the scope of the present study does not permit an exhaustive analysis of the Gospels, or even of the Gospel of John alone, as texts-in-performance. Yet it is possible and important at least to try to understand the Gospels as stories and the teaching of Jesus parallel in Matthew and Luke, that is "Q," as a series of speeches, and not just collections of individual sayings and mini-stories. As noted above and in earlier chapters, recent research on ancient communications culture and on texts-in-performance has shown that the still developing Gospel stories are in fact more stable and reliable sources for Jesus than the sayings and mini-stories whose wordings tended to be different from manuscript to manuscript. Even if we are not yet adequately prepared to appreciate the Gospel texts in performance, the approach taken here attempts to read the Gospels as whole stories that provide an overall sense of Jesus' mission and message as it developed in human interactions.

John's Story in Historical Context

CHAPTER FIVE

John's Story of Jesus

In Step II we summarized the plot of the Gospel of Mark as a historical story and "Q" as a series of Jesus' speeches and their portrayals of Jesus. Depending on the more extensive recent analysis of those Gospel sources, we now move into the relatively uncharted waters of reading the Gospel of John as a historical story in order to gain a sense of its portrayal of Jesus. The clear implication of the discussion in chapters 3 and 4 is that insofar as the Gospel of John is also a sustained story of Jesus, it stands on the same footing as the Synoptic Gospels as a source for our understanding of Jesus in historical context.

Rediscovery of John as a Story

The Gospel of John has long been understood as more theological than the Synoptic Gospels, and interpretation of the Gospel perpetuated this understanding. Important and influential interpretations of the Gospel of John in the 1950s and 1960s focused on its key themes and their development, viewing the Gospel as an expression of the "author's" ideology, more especially "his" Christology. While it was also a harbinger of the recent emphasis on John's whole story in its unified reading of the Gospel, C. H. Dodd's *Interpretation of the Fourth Gospel* in effect dissolved the story's sequence and movement into its theological themes.[1] On the premise that all of Jesus' actions and words in the Gospel were revelatory "signs" of Jesus' divine identity, Dodd found a close and essential correlation between the narrative sections and the discourse/dialogue sections, with the latter serving as the Evangelist's theological commentary on the significance of the former.[2] Indeed, Dodd understood each sign-discourse unit in the Gospel as an epitome of the totality of the early Christian proclamation.[3] The sequence did not really matter: John could have presented the events he describes in almost any order. Followed by Raymond Brown in his massive commentary and many others, Dodd's understanding of the Gospel as the development of theological themes dominated interpretation for decades and is still prominent. It was particularly important for theological education in showing how (the episodes in) the Gospel could lead the reader to faith, just as Jesus' signs and discourses led people to faith.

Like the other Gospels, however, the Gospel of John, was (re-)discovered as a sustained story starting in the 1970s. Reacting against earlier source-critical and developmental theories, interpreters began exploring the Gospel's narrative style, plot development, characterization, and use of various literary devices. Like the new literary criticism of Mark and the other Synoptic Gospels, analysis of John's narrative took its cues from criticism of modern fiction. It tended to treat the narrative world of John as self-contained, shaped by the literary and theological agenda of its "author," focusing on "the gospel as it stands rather than its sources,

---

1. C. H. Dodd, *The Interpretation of the Fourth Gospel* (Cambridge: Cambridge University Press, 1953). Dodd strongly influenced the also widely read commentary of Raymond Brown, *The Gospel According to John,* 2 vols. (Anchor Bible; New York: Doubleday, 1966, 1970). Their lasting influence is evident, for example, in Robert Kysar, *John: The Maverick Gospel,* 3rd ed. (Louisville: Westminster John Knox, 2007); D. Moody Smith, *John* (Abingdon New Testament Commentaries; Nashville: Abingdon, 1999); Jan van der Watt, *An Introduction to the Johannine Gospel and Letters* (Approaches to Biblical Studies; New York: T&T Clark, 2007); and Urban von Wahlde, *The Gospel and Letters of John,* 3 vols. (Eerdmans Critical Commentary; Grand Rapids: Eerdmans, 2010).

2. Dodd, *Interpretation of the Fourth Gospel,* 384, 451-52; and Dodd, *Historical Tradition in the Fourth Gospel* (Cambridge: Cambridge University Press, 1963), 54, 321, 354-55, 349-50 n. 1.

3. Dodd, *Interpretation of the Fourth Gospel,* 384.

historical background, or [theological] themes."[4] The new literary criticism of John has thus more or less deferred or avoided as irrelevant the story's relation to the historical world outside the text.[5]

The groundbreaking literary analysis of the Fourth Gospel was Alan Culpepper's *Anatomy of the Fourth Gospel,* which adapted various modes of literary criticism. Important for our consideration here are two of his closely interrelated conclusions: that the narrative (plot) is highly repetitive and that the Gospel's plot and characters are intertwined and mutually illuminating.[6] Since Jesus is a static character, a hero who cannot fail to fulfill his purposes, all depends on whether people will respond to his revelation with faith. Since each episode has essentially the same plot as the story as a whole, as Dodd noted, the story is repeated over and over as Jesus meets new people. Every episode has more or less the same narrative function, providing Jesus an occasion for his revelation. With this reading of the Gospel as a series of repetitive episodes consisting of narrated signs and attached discourses/dialogues that have no clear sequence and could be arranged in almost any order, Culpepper has thus not moved the understanding of John's story far beyond its interpretation in terms of theological themes.

Other literary critics, however, began to notice other features of John's story. Particularly important was the recognition of Jesus' journeys from area to area and place to place in the narrative and of how those journeys are articulated together with the various festivals celebrated in the Jerusalem temple.[7]

Insofar as literary critics of John often think in terms of the closed world within the text, as in current criticism of modern fiction, they often couch their observations in metaphors borrowed from modern

---

4. Quoting R. Alan Culpepper, *Anatomy of the Fourth Gospel: A Study in Literary Design* (Philadelphia: Fortress, 1983), 5.

5. On the "eclipse" of the historical context of Jesus and of the Gospel story in Johannine studies, see Tom Thatcher, "Anatomies of the Fourth Gospel: Past, Present, and Future Probes," in *Anatomies of Narrative Criticism: The Past, Present, and Futures of the Fourth Gospel as Literature,* ed. Tom Thatcher and Stephen Moore (Resources for Biblical Study 55; Atlanta: Society of Biblical Literature, 2008), 2-17.

6. Culpepper, *Anatomy,* chapter 4.

7. See especially Fernando Segovia, "The Journeys of the Word of God: A Reading of the Plot of the Fourth Gospel," *Semeia* 53 (1991), 27-45.

readers' experience in modern print culture. Central to our agenda here is to appreciate the story of John's Gospel rather in the ancient media context, long before the advent of print culture. Calling attention to Jesus' movement from area to area in connection with the festivals in the temple leads to the necessary further recognition that, like the other Gospels, the Gospel of John is a historical story. In the climax of the story, Jesus is handed over by Caiaphas and is crucified by order of the Roman governor Pontius Pilate, both of whom are known from other sources to have been in office simultaneously. The story is about Jesus' interaction with people and their rulers that result in his execution. The "prologue" to the story (1:1-18), moreover, while clearly a theological poem, declares as its main point that in Jesus the Logos was "made flesh," that is, became a human person, a historical actor. It seems obvious that if we are to honor the literary (and theological) integrity of the story, we must recognize and consider it as a historical story set in a historical context.

John as a Historical Story

As with our sample reading in chapter 3, to better appreciate the Gospel's historical story of Jesus it may help to focus initially on the three interrelated fundamental features of a story: setting, characters, and plot. Obviously, these features are inseparable in any story; we treat them individually here with a view to emphasizing how each contributes to understanding John as a historical narrative and, ultimately, a source for Jesus. These analytical steps will be oversimplifications. But taking them may help us cut through the all too familiar previous reading of John's story through standard concepts such as "(early) Judaism," "(early) Christianity," "theology," and "Christology" that obscure what is happening in the story as the conflict among the main characters intensifies, leading to the crucifixion of Jesus.

Because the previously standard understanding of the Gospel of John has been predominantly in terms of its themes and structure, however, it is important to recognize at the outset the difference between an outline of a book and the plot of a story. A plot (often with interwoven subplots) develops in a sequence of interrelated events that have consequences, that lead to subsequent events, and eventually to climactic events (usually at the end). As a story proceeds, the events often involve recognitions and/or reversals. It is fair to say that most "outlines" of the Fourth Gospel have focused primarily on its development of symbolic networks or theological themes, not on its patterns of conflict and certainly not on correlation with the historical context. In the following discussion any reference to "structure" or "pattern" or "outline" refers not to the Gospel's theological or symbolic development, but rather to the plot of the story and its portrayal of Jesus in interaction. To enhance appreciation of how the story unfolds, we urge readers, even those familiar with the Gospel, to pause at this point to read quickly through the text, preferably in a presentation lacking indications of chapter and verse and subtitles of paragraphs.

Setting

As noted in Chapter 3, one key to Mark's story lies in the contrast between the villages of Galilee (and nearby areas), where Jesus carries out most of his mission, and Jerusalem, where he confronts the rulers and, consequently, is crucified. In John's story the settings are more complex, as Jesus moves from place to place and region to region, and thus all the more important to the unfolding plot. Most notably John has Jesus go up to Jerusalem specifically at times of festivals in the temple, such as Passover. Following the changes of setting, as Jesus moves from one or another of the rural regions to Jerusalem and then back to one of those regions, is key to following the story of intensifying conflict.

Jesus begins his public activity, performing his first "sign," in the village of Cana in Galilee, his home country (*patris,* John 4:43-45), but immediately goes "up to Jerusalem" for the Passover festival of the Judeans, where he carries out an attack on business in the temple (2:1-11, 12-22). After his conversation with the Pharisee Nicodemus ("a ruler of the Judeans"), Jesus spends some time in the countryside of Judea (3:1-21, 22-36). Then, on his way back from Judea to Galilee, he goes through Samaria, where he converses with the Samaritan woman at the well and other Samaritans (4:1-42). Once back in Galilee, Jesus pronounces a royal official's son healed (4:43-54), his second Cana "sign," but soon returns to Jerusalem for another festival of the Judeans. There he heals a paralyzed man on the Sabbath, which leads to the Judeans' resolve to kill him and the first of his extended discussions with them (5:1-47).

Jesus then goes to "the other side of the Sea of Galilee," where on a mountain at the time of Passover he feeds a multitude before returning back across the Sea to Capernaum (6:1-71). Reluctant to travel to Jerusalem again for the festival of Booths, realizing that the Judeans want to kill him, Jesus eventually goes up secretly and begins to teach publicly in the temple; confirming his fears, the high priests and Pharisees attempt to arrest him (7:1-52). He continues to teach in (the treasury of) the temple until he is about to be stoned, then he heals a blind man, leading to a further heated dispute (8:12-59; 9:1-41). Still in Jerusalem for the festival of Dedication, he is almost stoned again, whereupon he goes away again "across the Jordan" (10:22-42).

Over the protests of the disciples about the very real threat of death, Jesus goes again into Judea to heal Lazarus, which leads the high priests and Pharisees to plot how to put him to death (11:1-44, 45-53). He withdraws again to a village in the Judean wilderness, then returns to Lazarus's home in Bethany a week before Passover; from there he enters Jerusalem once again, this time to the popular acclamations of a great crowd (11:54–12:19). The climax of the story, including Jesus' footwashing at the meal, his long "farewell" discourse with his disciples, and his arrest, hearing before Pilate, crucifixion, and resurrection, is set in Jerusalem. If John 21 is included in the story, the resurrected Jesus returns to his homeland of Galilee for a final meeting with the disciples.

Whereas in Mark only the climactic events take place in Jerusalem, in John much of Jesus' action and all his increasingly rancorous debates with the Judean scribal class take place in the temple in Jerusalem. The other regions of his activity, however, are important not only as places where he retreats from the danger of being killed in Jerusalem, but as places where he carries out signs and other actions. In all the regions Jesus visits, moreover, "many trust in him" as a result of his activity.

Characters

In contrast to modern novels, ancient stories do not "develop" character(s), as noted in chapter 3. The main characters in John's story, more than in other ancient stories, including the Synoptic Gospels, are types, even stereotypes.[8] One of the ways in which the gospel stories differ the most from modern narrative fiction is that many of the characters are not (so much) individual people with distinctive personalities as people serving in institutionalized positions and functions or, at the popular level, people acting in roles rooted in Israelite tradition or representatives of a whole group of people. These characters in the story, moreover, usually do not act and speak individually but collectively or representatively.

Indeed, such are the principal characters in John's story, who quickly become engaged in the story's main conflict: Jesus, the high priests, and, at the end of the story, Pontius Pilate. While John's main characters in some ways demonstrate greater depth than their Synoptic counterparts, they show very little development, instead performing relatively stereotyped and predictable roles.

Even before John's story proper really begins, the main character Jesus has already been declared to be "the Messiah," "the Son of God, the King of Israel" — indeed, Mr. Everything in Israelite tradition. In the introductory "prologue" (1:1-18) and sequence of encounters (vv. 19-51), Andrew and Nathanael, along with others who are soon to become disciples, acclaim Jesus with titles and roles of long-anticipated salvific figures of Israelite cultural tradition. Most important is "the Messiah" (often synonymous with "the Son of God"/"the king of Israel"), which is the principal identity of Jesus and the role discussed in questions about him ("are you the . . . ?" "can this be the . . . ?") or asserted of him at many points throughout the story (1:18, 41, 49; 4:25, 29; 7:26-27, 31, 41-42; 9:22; 10:24; 11:27, etc.). Indeed, the purpose in "writing" the many "signs" that Jesus performed is to enable the audience to trust that Jesus is "the Messiah, the Son of God" and to have life in his name (20:30-31). "Son of Man"

---

8. The term "flat character," coined by E. M. Forster, *Aspects of the Novel* (New York: Harcourt, Brace & World, 1954), 103-18, was popularized in Johannine Studies by Culpepper, *Anatomy*, especially 102-3.

is the title/role for the one who mediates life and salvation between God and people, heaven and earth (1:51; 6:27, 62). A series of references to his being "lifted up" points to the way he will die, by being "lifted up" on the cross (3:13-14; 8:28; 12:31-34), which paradoxically is also his "glorification" (12:23). "A/the prophet," while much less prominent in the story as a title of Jesus, is the role in which he acts and speaks in many of the episodes (1:21, 25; 4:19; 6:14; 7:40, 52; 9:17). Throughout John's story, the "larger-than-life" main character Jesus acts and speaks with full authority and in serene control of events, especially when confronting the high priests and Pharisees and when confronted by Pilate.

The other main characters, whom Jesus engages in repeated and escalating confrontations, are the collective "high priests and Pharisees," who are sometimes referred to (interchangeably) as "the Judeans." In view of the tragic long-standing tradition of translating the Greek term *hoi Ioudaioi* ("the Judeans") as "the Jews," as understood in relation to the synthetic Christian construct of "Judaism," it is important to be clear about who "the Judeans" are in John's narrative. Who is included in the term is not always the same. The starting point toward clarity, context by context in the course of the story, is surely to recognize that "Judea," "Galilee," and "Samaria" are regional terms, references to particular areas or districts of Roman Palestine where the people were of Israelite heritage. The corresponding terms for people, "the Judeans," "the Galileans," and "the Samaritans" are, similarly, regional references to the people of the respective areas or districts. However, at most points in the conflictual debates of the Gospel and in Jesus' arrest, his hearing before Pilate, and the crucifixion scene, "the Judeans" are clearly synonymous with "the high priests and the Pharisees." Just as "the Americans" or "the Russians" are often used in reference to the government of the United States or Russia, so "the Judeans" in John often refers to the rulers of the Judeans. On the other hand, in certain other contexts, such as when Jesus goes into the countryside of Judea, "the Judeans" who trust in him are Judean villagers. Understanding the story in general and the identity of "the Judeans" thus involves attention to the context, including the particular setting. Virtually throughout John's story, "the Judeans" as the high priests and the Pharisees are opposed by and opposed to Jesus in the story's dominant conflict.

Comparison of the roles of the high priests and the Pharisees in John with their roles in Mark helps illuminate these characters' function in John's story. While the Pharisees (along with the scribes) speak and act more as the representatives of the high priests in Mark, they (with no mention of "the scribes") work closely in tandem with the high priests in John. John's story, moreover, presents the high priests (and Pharisees) as fearful of the reaction of the Romans, hence acting in close collaboration with the governor, insisting that "we have no king but Caesar!" (19:15).

Interrelated with the characters of the dominant conflict are numerous other characters. In the final episodes in Jerusalem, the Roman governor Pilate, responding to the insistence of the high priests, finally orders Jesus to be crucified. Frequently God the Father is pointedly present as the main actor in Jesus' discourses. The Spirit also plays a role, particularly in Jesus' long final discourse. The disciples collectively and particular disciples play intermediate roles throughout the story, including in Jesus' long discourse prior to his arrest, trial, and crucifixion. Also important, in measuring the effects of Jesus' actions, are the anonymous crowds of the various regions — Galileans, Samaritans, Judeans, and those across the Jordan — who come to "trust in him." The crowds and the people whom Jesus heals play cameo roles. And it is important to the story to mention particular representative figures from each region: Peter, the Beloved Disciple, and Nathanael in Galilee; the woman at the well in Samaria; Mary, Martha, and Lazarus in Judea; and Nicodemus in Jerusalem.

Plot

As noted in Chapter 3, the plot of a story is integrally related to its dominant conflict. While plots may follow temporal or geographical sequences and may develop symbolic and thematic networks, these sequences and networks do not constitute a plot. A plot, rather, is a series of events that move the story along to a climactic main conflict, sometimes also but not always to the story's resolution.[9]

9. Seymour Chatman, whose work has been foundational to narrative criticism of all the Gospels, calls the events indispensable to a story's progress "kernels" (*Story and Discourse: Narrative Structure in Fiction and Film* [Ithaca: Cornell University Press, 1978], 53-56).

As in Mark's story, John's dominant conflict is between Jesus and the "Judean" heads of the temple in Jerusalem (under the oversight of the Roman governor Pilate). But this is much more evident and dramatic virtually from the outset of John than in Mark. No sooner has Jesus appeared in Galilee in John's story than he goes up to Jerusalem at the Passover festival of the Judeans and forcibly blockades normal business in the temple, an action that occurs much later in Mark's story as the beginning of the climactic confrontations in Jerusalem (John 2:12-22; Mark 11:12-17). In John, moreover, this most blatant confrontation in the temple is only the first in a series of confrontations that he initiates by some action at one or another of the "festivals of the Judeans" in the temple. He goes up to Jerusalem again on the occasion of "a festival of the Judeans" where he pointedly does a healing on the Sabbath, for which "the Judeans" try to kill him for an act against their law (5:1-18). Again he goes up to Jerusalem during "the Judeans' festival of Booths" to teach in the temple, where the continuing dispute over his healing on the Sabbath leads to another attempt by "the Judeans"/the Pharisees to have him arrested (7:1-32). Again at the festival of Dedication, the continuing dispute leads to "the Judeans'" attempt to stone him or arrest him (10:22-39). His ascent up to Jerusalem at another Passover, acclaimed as "the king of Israel," finally leads the high priests and Pharisees to take decisive action to arrest him for fear the Romans will crack down on the significant unrest he is stirring up (11:47-53; 12:12-19; 18:1-14).

The core of the plot of the Gospel is thus that Jesus, as the agent provocateur, carries out a series of sustained confrontations of the rulers of the Judeans and what they represent in the Jerusalem temple-state, who finally succeed in arresting him and hand him over to the Roman governor, who executes him. The plot of the Gospel, however, is more complicated, as it steadily "thickens" in the unfolding of the story. Not only does Jesus perform his provocative actions in Jerusalem at festival times as attacks on the temple, its rulers, and its restrictive law, but he also performs his actions in Galilee as pointed alternatives to the practices of the Jerusalem temple-state. In the very first act of his mission, at the wedding feast in Cana of Galilee, Jesus uses six stone jars "for the purification rites of the Judeans" for the water that he changes into wine, using them for a purpose pointedly opposed to that for which they were intended by "the Judeans" (from up there in Jerusalem, 2:1-11). Again several episodes later, pointedly just as "the Passover, the festival of the Judeans," approaches, he crosses to the other side of the Sea of Galilee and performs the feeding of the multitude on the mountain (6:1-14). Similarly in Samaria, in his conversation with the woman at the well, Jesus' declaration about worship of God is an alternative to, and rejection of, the temple in Jerusalem (4:23-24).

Throughout the story, Jesus' actions and statements in the role of a/ the prophet or "the Messiah" are thus an alternative to as well as in opposition to the temple-state in Jerusalem. Also, throughout the narrative both Jesus' actions and his statements are heavily symbolic, with rich allusions to Israelite tradition, suggesting that his acts and words and he himself are the fulfillment of the people's longings and eager expectations. The "red thread" or the "axis" of the plot that runs through the Gospel story is thus not just Jesus' confrontations with the Judean rulers in Jerusalem, but the opposition that Jesus acts out in his prophetic and messianic roles between the Jerusalem rulers and the people in all the regions of Israelite heritage and in Jerusalem itself.

Moreover, Jesus performs these actions, the healings in Jerusalem, and many other actions in Jerusalem and in the countryside of Galilee, Judea, and Samaria as "signs" for the people, in response to which they come "to trust in him/his name" (2:11, 23, etc.; the standard English translation "believe in" diminishes the force of the Greek term for "trust in" in the sense of "be loyal to," a term the Romans used for political loyalty and commitment). Because of the many signs that Jesus performs, or because of his word or the testimony of the Samaritan woman or other figures, many people trust in/become loyal to Jesus. Through the course of the story, beginning with the disciples in Cana of Galilee, this happens with many in Jerusalem (2:23; 7:31), in Samaria (4:39-42), the royal official back in Galilee (4:46-54), many in the area across the Jordan (10:40-42), and many in Judea outside Jerusalem (11:45) — that is, in all the regions of Israelite heritage and in the Judean capital city as well. What have unusually not been noted, probably because the story is usually read narrowly as a mainly religious story, are the political implications of this expanding response of trust in/loyalty to Jesus. As the movement expands dramatically in rural Judea in response to the sign of the raising of Lazarus, John has the high priests and Pharisees exclaim explicitly, "This man is performing many signs. If we let him go on like this, everyone will become loyal to him" — and evoke a Roman crackdown (11:45-48).

What the "signs" and the response to them thus indicate is that a widening movement has been gathering around Jesus. This, however, has been happening not just in the course of the series of confrontations that Jesus has provoked with the Jerusalem rulers in the temple at times of the festivals of the Judeans, but at other times and places in the story as well. Not usually noticed in the story, probably because of the standard focus on theological themes and Jesus' discourses, is that Jesus spends time also in the countryside of all of the regions of Israelite heritage, Galilee, Samaria, Judea, and the region across the Jordan. And as stated explicitly in the narrative, in all those regions, "many" became loyal to him. Thus in John's story as well as Mark's, the plot includes Jesus' forming and leading a movement. But whereas Mark has the movement focused in Galilee and surrounding regions, John has the movement developing in all of the regions of Israelite heritage. If we have "ears to hear" John's story, it seems that the plot includes not just the series of Jesus' confrontations of the Jerusalem rulers that leads inexorably to his crucifixion, but also his evoking a popular movement of renewal of the people of Israel in opposition to and by the rulers. While telling a story that seems, on the surface, to be quite different from Mark's, with long discourses and the major confrontation at the beginning, John presents a plot that is very similar to Mark's. While Mark's plot has Jesus catalyzing the renewal of Israel in opposition to and by the rulers of Israel, John's plot has Jesus repeatedly confronting the rulers of Israel as he catalyzes a renewal of Israel.

John's Portrayal of Jesus

With this rough grasp of the setting, characters, and plot of the Gospel of John we can sketch a summary of the story, looking for how the Gospel portrays Jesus' conflict with the rulers in Jerusalem and the people's response to him in the various regions. Because the narrative in John is often highly symbolic, particularly in references to Israelite tradition, it will be important to attend to such references and overtones.

Even before Jesus begins his action in Galilee, John's baptism is evidently threatening to the rulers in Jerusalem. The Pharisees send a delegation to closely interrogate John as to whether he is (the expected) "Elijah" or "the prophet" (1:19-28). Especially in Israelite tradition, the activity of a prophet in the wilderness posed a threat to the Jerusalem rulers. The immediately ensuing identification of Jesus as fulfilling all the expected roles of agents of liberation and renewal of Israel, however, indicates that he is the one who will mount the opposition and renewal (on these titles and roles, see further chapter 7 below).

Jesus commences his action in the village of Cana in Galilee, his ancestral homeland (4:44). The portrayal of his first "sign" is highly symbolic of the new life in fulfillment of Israelite tradition that Jesus is bringing. This episode is typical of John's narrative in the heavy overlay of symbolism and references to Israelite tradition and tradition about Jesus. "On the third day" is an obvious allusion to the resurrection of Jesus and the new life it has brought to the people. In contrast to modern theological narrowing to the resuscitation of an individual body, what has come to be called "resurrection" symbolism was always an anticipation of a collective "corporate" restoration or renewal of the people (as symbolized again in the sign of the raising of Lazarus: "the resurrection and the life"). The "wedding" was traditionally a (albeit patriarchal) symbol of the intimate bond between God and the people. And as just noted, in appropriating the stone jars dedicated to "the Judeans' rites of purification," Jesus clearly signals the arrival of a new political-economic-religious order alternative to the one headed by "the Judeans," an order that operates for the family and community life of the people in the villages.

The story immediately juxtaposes the new life in Cana with the ruling institution of the temple in Jerusalem and its operation as a "marketplace" for the benefit of the ruling elite (2:12-16). Jesus takes obstructive action against the temple at "the Passover of the Judeans," which may have been the most salient symbol of the temple as the ruling political-economic-religious institution. Passover was the celebration of the exodus liberation of the people of Israel from foreign domination and exploitation in Egypt. In early Israelite tradition, Passover was celebrated locally in the constituent families of Israel. Centuries before the time of Jesus, however, it had been centralized in the Jerusalem temple. This was part of the centralization of political-economic-religious power in the Judean temple-state. That is, instead of consuming their Passover lambs and other produce locally, the people were required to sell produce for coins and then buy animals (at markup) suitable to be sacrificed in the temple, where the priests would receive choice cuts.

Jesus' forcible obstruction of the temple market — hardly a "reform," much less a "cleansing" — serves as a prophetic demonstration that enacts his/God's condemnation of the whole ruling institution, its apparatus, and its imperial connections. Jesus' declaration ("word," 2:19-22) suggests that the Jerusalem rulers have been "destroying" the "temple"; in "three days," however, Jesus will "raise it up," another obvious reference to the forthcoming resurrection of the "temple" of Jesus' body, which represented new life for the people (or the people itself). That deliverance and new life for (or the renewal of) the people under the direct "kingdom/rule of God" is what Jesus was doing in the obstruction of the temple business is further underscored by the cryptic and scoffing debate with the Pharisee Nicodemus, a representative "ruler of the Judeans."

Jesus' next action (John 3:22-36), often overlooked because of its proximity to the famous dialogue with Nicodemus and subsequent theological summary of Jesus' ministry (vv. 1-21), is integral to the developing conflict in the Gospel's story. "Jesus and (assisted by?) his disciples went into the Judean countryside, and he spent some time with them and he baptized." What is more, Jesus' work in the countryside of Judea, where John had been baptizing as well, outstripped the movement of his prophetic predecessor to such an extent that "the Judeans" were worried that "all were going to him." Again in the early episodes of John's story, as in Mark's, it is clear that Jesus was working among the villagers and generating a movement.

In John's Gospel, however, Jesus' mission extends to all areas of Israelite heritage, most dramatically in the next episode, which is unique to John's Gospel (4:1-42). Knowing that the Pharisees (working closely in tandem with the high priests as "the Judeans") were after him, Jesus "left Judea and started back to Galilee." On his way through Samaria he stops at Sychar, the ground that Jacob, the eponymous ancestor of all Israel, had given to the (traditionally largest and central) tribe of Joseph, he encounters a Samaritan woman at Jacob's well. In their allusive step-by-step dialogue Jesus declares that God will be worshiped neither on "this mountain" (Mount Gerizim, where the Judean high priesthood had destroyed the Samaritan temple) nor in the temple in Jerusalem and that he is (a) messiah whom the woman knows is coming. From this it could not be clearer that Jesus and his mission are bringing a new order for the people of Israel. After Jesus exhorts his disciples that "the fields are ripe for harvesting," "many" and then "many more" Samaritans trust in/become loyal to Jesus. By the conclusion of the fourth episode in the story, then, John has Jesus working among the people, generating a movement in the three main regions of Israelite heritage, and attacking the ruling institution of the temple in Jerusalem.

After he returns to Jerusalem at another "festival of the Judeans," at the pool of Bethzatha, by which lay many blind, lame, and paralyzed people, Jesus commands a crippled man who has lain there "for thirty-eight years" to "stand up, take your mat, and walk," thus healing him on the Sabbath (5:1-24). On learning that Jesus has healed the man, the Judeans seek to kill him; Jesus justifies his actions by insisting that since "my Father" is working all the time (including on the Sabbath), he himself is working to give life to the people. Addressing their charge that Sabbath healing violates the Law, Jesus challenges their reliance on their "Scripture," insisting that Moses in fact "wrote" about him (5:45-47).

Back in Galilee, Jesus crosses the lake with a large crowd following him because they saw the signs he was doing for the sick. There he feeds a multitude on the mountain (6:1-24). Following the sign, the disciples "assemble" (same root as "synagogue," the assembly of a village community or of the whole people) "the fragments" left over, which filled twelve baskets. This "sign" was clearly a feeding symbolic of the assembling of the renewed people of Israel, timed pointedly to serve as an alternative to the Passover of the Judeans in Jerusalem (v. 4). The people know that "this is indeed the prophet who is to come" (v. 14). Compounding the role of the prophet they see him as fulfilling, they seek "to make him king" as well, whereupon Jesus withdraws back across the lake to Capernaum. This sets up Jesus' declaration, referring to the manna that God gave the Israelites in the wilderness, that he is the bread from heaven that gives life, referring again to his coming crucifixion.

The introduction to the next episode states explicitly that the conflict between Jesus and the Judean rulers has intensified as a result of his previous provocations. Knowing that the Judeans are looking for an opportunity to do away with him and are keeping close surveillance, Jesus is reluctant to return to Jerusalem at the festival of Booths even though his brothers challenge him to publicly expand the works he is doing (7:1-13). Jesus finally does go up, secretly, but then, brazenly teaching in the temple, disputes the Judeans' inconsistent interpretation of the Law with regard to his earlier Sabbath healing, leading many to speculate that he must be the Messiah. The situation in Jerusalem has become politically explosive. The high priests and Pharisees send "servants" (guards, the "temple-police") to arrest Jesus, while the crowd debates whether he might be "the prophet" or "the Messiah," an impossible proposition in the minds of the rulers because the Judean Scriptures say that the Messiah is the descendant of David and therefore must come from Bethlehem (vv. 32-52). The guards, however, impressed at the authority with which Jesus speaks, fail to arrest him, utterly flabbergasting the high priestly rulers and Pharisees. The latter betray their own arrogant disdain of the populace, whom they view as "accursed" because they do not know the Law (= the great Judean tradition which they themselves control), expressing particular disregard for Galileans. Indeed, "no prophet rises up from Galilee" (7:52).

Jesus' reappearance in the temple treasury further exposes the misunderstanding of the Pharisees about his mediation of life to the people (8:12-59). He disputes the Judeans' inconsistency in their understanding and application of their law. Jesus' affirmation to the Judeans who have trusted in him that those who know the truth would be "freed" by it, a term often used for freedom from the Romans or other imperial power, serves as a foil for another dispute about whether they are or are not the children of Abraham, with Jesus ultimately claiming precedence/superiority over their revered ancestor. The debate degenerates into an attempted stoning and Jesus exits.

As he leaves the temple complex, Jesus punctuates his earlier points with another Sabbath healing, this time of a blind man. As with the Bethzatha healing, this act provokes an inquiry by the Pharisees, revealing the sharp divide that has developed between those who trust in Jesus, whom the Judean rulers have resolved to expel from the assembly (of the Judean people, 9:22), and the Pharisees, who claim to be "disciples of

Moses" (vv. 1-34). Jesus now clearly has an expanding following, including some secret sympathizers among the people of Jerusalem as well as villagers in the different rural regions. The Judeans' expulsion (from the people) of the healed man, who had become a disciple of Jesus, prompts Jesus to declare that he himself is the gate of the sheepfold as well as the good "shepherd" who lays down his life for the sheep, who hear his voice and follow him (10:1-18). There can be no question but that these remarks are offered as a specific condemnation of the Judean rulers, who are in fact the target audience of Jesus' discourse (9:40-41). When Jesus appears again in the temple at the festival of Dedication, the Judean rulers accuse him of blasphemy and attempt to stone him. Jesus appeals to their law against them, then flees across the Jordan, where, again, "many become loyal to him" (10:22-42).

The next two episodes, the most ominous since Jesus' attack on the temple, bring the intensifying conflict to a head. In both, the narrative weaves together a number of threads of the story. In the first, Jesus hears from the sisters Mary and Martha, residents of Bethany (two miles from Jerusalem) and apparently prominent figures in the nascent movement in Judea, that their brother Lazarus is sick (11:1-44). Over the objections of the disciples that any return to the neighborhood of Jerusalem is suicide, Jesus decides to go to his friends' house, but delays arrival until Lazarus has been four days in the tomb. Jesus arrives at the village to discover that many Judeans from Jerusalem have come to mourn with Mary and Martha. In a short dialogue, Jesus declares "'I am' the resurrection and the life," and Martha declares that he is "the Messiah, the Son of God." The narrative thus has Jesus acting as "the Messiah" in raising Lazarus, though perhaps also with undertones of the prophet Elijah and his protégé Elisha, who were the ones known from Israelite tradition to have raised the dead as part of the renewal of Israel (1 Kgs 17:17-24; 2 Kgs 4:17-37). Taken to the tomb by Mary and the Judeans, Jesus commands, "Lazarus, come out!" Lazarus obeys, leading many of the Judeans who have come with Mary to become loyal to Jesus, while others go off to inform the Pharisees of what has happened (John 11:46).

The raising of Lazarus leads directly to the narrative's most explicit statement of what is happening in the story (11:46-53). Convening a meeting of the council, the high priests and Pharisees see the acute political crisis that has come to a head, with ominous implications for their own position of power in the imperial order. "This man is performing many signs. If we let him go on like this, everyone will become loyal to him, and the Romans will come and destroy both our holy place and our people." The high priest Caiaphas discerns what they must do in their position as Roman client rulers: "it is better for you to have one man die for the people *(laos)* than to have the whole nation *(ethnos)* destroyed." The narrative ameliorates the coldness of this logic somewhat by interpreting Caiaphas's words as a prophecy "that Jesus was about to die for the people . . . and to gather into one the dispersed children of God." The council forms a plan to put Jesus to death, while he withdraws to the village of Ephraim toward the wilderness (11:54).

Now the conflict moves to the final ominous confrontation (11:54-57; 12:1-19). As the Passover approaches, villagers who have come up from the country to prepare for the festival look for Jesus in Jerusalem, apparently expecting that he will appear, while the Pharisees keep the situation under surveillance (11:55-57). Shortly before Passover, Jesus returns to Bethany, where Mary anoints his feet, an act that Jesus explicitly associates with his own impending death and burial (12:1-8). As word of Jesus' presence spreads, crowds of Judeans come to Bethany to see both him and Lazarus, the latter now also targeted for execution by the high priests in view of the fact "many of the Judeans were deserting and becoming loyal to Jesus" because of Lazarus's resurrection (12:9-11). The great crowd that has come to the festival, learning that Jesus was coming to Jerusalem, goes out to greet him, waving branches of palm trees and hailing him as "the king of Israel," a title/role that Jesus seems to tacitly affirm by entering the city on a donkey in fulfillment of the prophecy of the coming of a popular king from Israelite tradition (Zech 9:9). Converging with this great crowd of country people in Jerusalem for the Passover is the crowd of those (Judeans) who were with Jesus when he called Lazarus out of the tomb. In apparent despair, the Pharisees rightly observe to one another, "You see, you can do nothing. Look, the world has gone after him" (12:19).

In addition to having generated a movement of loyalists rooted in the villages of Galilee, Samaria, the Transjordan, and Judea, Jesus is now at the center of a nonviolent insurrection of Judeans from the country along with Judeans from Jerusalem at the Passover celebration of the liberation of the people. He is, however, aware of just how he will die: he will be raised up from the earth on a cross (12:20-36). Yet he prophesies that his imminent crucifixion is also the time of the world's judgment: "the ruler of the world (Rome, Caesar) will be driven out."[10] Jesus flees into hiding. Meanwhile many of "the rulers/authorities" become loyal to him, but secretly for fear that the Pharisees will expel them from (the assembly of) the people (12:36-43).

Following Jesus' washing of the disciples' feet and his lengthy discourse on the tight bond of love (solidarity) between himself, the Father, and the community and his promise to send the Spirit, action resumes with the implementation of the plan to arrest and execute Jesus. Unlike the Synoptics' Gethsemane scene, Jesus remains serene throughout, in seeming command of the situation. The betrayer Judas brings a joint force of Roman soldiers and "servants" (guards) from the high priests and Pharisees to arrest Jesus in a garden outside the city. Jesus in no way resists, instead boldly identifying himself to the posse and criticizing Peter's violent attempt to protect him (18:1-11).

The so-called "trial(s)" of Jesus before the high priest and Pilate offer a vivid example of the mutual maneuverings by which the Roman governor and the client rulers in the Jerusalem temple-state sought to control affairs in Judea. The high priest's interrogation of Jesus seeks to ferret out information about the extent, organization, and ideology of Jesus' movement. Jesus responds that such information is common knowledge, for he himself has always taught publicly ("in assembly" = openly) everywhere he went, including the temple (18:19-23). The high priests take Jesus to the Roman governor, Pontius Pilate, and demand his execution. When the suspicious Pilate tells them to "judge him according to your law," the Judean rulers remind him that the Romans retain the power of execution (vv. 28-31). Pilate's questioning of Jesus, full of ironies and double entendres, focuses on the question of Jesus' "kingship." Jesus insists that "my kingdom is not of this world," that is, not the Roman imperial order. But of course that is just the problem, both for Pilate and for the

---

10. For further discussion, see Tom Thatcher, *Greater Than Caesar: Christology and Empire in the Fourth Gospel* (Minneapolis: Fortress, 2009), 116-22.

Judean high priests, as the preceding narrative has shown: Jesus' actions and speeches have become ever more subversive of the order they were both responsible for maintaining in Judea. And although, as clearly stated at two key points earlier in the story, Jesus' followers acclaimed him "the king of *Israel*," from the Roman governor's point of view any person who claims a "kingdom" in connection with a challenge to the imperial order in Judea is posing as "the king of the *Judeans*" (Herod the Great's former title) — that is, as a threat to the imperium of Caesar. In point of fact, Pilate's hesitance to condemn Jesus seems to reflect not only his desire to capitalize on the political potential of Jesus' case, but also his genuine "outsider" confusion about the inherent differences between a prophet and an insurrectionary king. Throughout the hearing, the Judean rulers consistently interpret Jesus' movement in political terms that Pilate can understand, with the result that Jesus is ultimately condemned as "king of the Judeans," a title he has never claimed but that is posted over him on the cross as grounds for his death.

After having Jesus tortured, Pilate insists that he finds nothing culpable in him (19:1-16). The Judean rulers respond by taking the conversation in a new direction: Jesus deserves to die not only because he claimed to be "king of the Judeans" but also because he postures himself as "Son of God," a principal title of the Roman emperor. More apprehensive than ever, Pilate tries to release Jesus, but the Judean rulers further manipulate him with the fawning declaration that "we have no king but Caesar." This concession, which Pilate could only interpret as a political victory, is accompanied by a lightly-veiled threat: "If you do not get rid of him, you are no friend of Caesar." Realizing the implications of their insinuation and satisfied that he has sufficiently humiliated both Jesus and the priests, Pilate hands Jesus over for execution.

The crucifixion scene is then the occasion for the dying Jesus to commend the care of his mother to the disciple whom he loved. The ensuing details of the crucifixion are done in fulfillment of a number of prophecies from the Judean Scriptures. Joseph of Arimathea, a secret disciple of Jesus from among the rulers, assisted by another ruler, Nicodemus, who has also evidently become a follower, give Jesus an honorable burial in a new tomb (19:17-42).

The story, of course, does not end with the crucifixion. On the first day of the week, Mary Magdalene, Peter, and the Beloved Disciple find the tomb empty (20:1-9). The resurrected Jesus appears to Mary (vv. 11-18), then to the disciples, who are meeting behind locked doors for fear of arrest by the Judeans, and breathes on them to mediate their reception of the promised Holy Spirit (vv. 19-23), which will empower their "witness" and thus the continuation of his renewal movement. If John 21 is included in the story, it anticipates the further expansion of Jesus' movement among the Galilean villages, where Jesus appears to several of his disciples one last time by the lake.

CHAPTER SIX

Verisimilitude vs. Verification

———— ⌾⌾⌾ ————

The Gospel of John not only tells a historical story. It also has historical credibility in the broad sense that it fits the historical situation in which it is set as that situation can be known from other sources.[1] While the Gospel is by no means a critical history book, it does have considerable historical verisimilitude. We look here mainly for the general fit of John's narrative with the fundamental political-economic structure and dynamics, the regional differences, and the cultural divide sketched in chapters 1 and 2, along with some further particulars.

The Rulers and the People

Most striking, surely, is how John's story, like the other Gospel stories, portrays the fundamental divide between the rulers resident in the cities and the vast majority of people living in village communities in Roman Palestine, as represented in Judean sources such as the histories of Josephus

---

1. For how the historical context of Jesus and John's Gospel has been "eclipsed" by attention to the narrative, see Tom Thatcher, "Anatomies of the Fourth Gospel: Past, Present, and Future Probes," in *Anatomies of Narrative Criticism: The Past, Present, and Futures of the Fourth Gospel as Literature,* ed. Tom Thatcher and Stephen Moore (Resources for Biblical Study 55; Atlanta: Society of Biblical Literature, 2008), 2-17.

and the earlier instructional speeches of Ben Sira. In just that historical context, moreover, the Gospel of John presents Jesus as a prophet and a messiah leading a movement of villagers against the Jerusalem rulers and their Roman patrons in terms parallel to the closely contemporary popular prophets and popular messiahs in Josephus's accounts.

On the underside of the divide, in John as well as in extra-Gospel sources, are the ordinary people of the countryside in their towns and villages along with the ordinary people of Jerusalem. John leaves no doubt that it was mainly in the countryside villages where Jesus interacted with the people, "many" of whom came to trust in him. John also leaves no doubt that the Galileans, the Samaritans, and the Judeans who became loyal to Jesus were villagers. The story makes a special note of priests, scribal teachers, Pharisees such as Nicodemus, or other elite figures such as the Herodian ("royal") official in Galilee and even some of "the rulers," who came to trust in Jesus (e.g., 4:46-54; 12:42). Otherwise, those who became loyal to Jesus were mainly people in the countryside of the different areas.

Insofar as John focuses most of Jesus' action and discourse in Jerusalem and the temple, the story makes far fewer references to villages than do either the Synoptic Gospels or Josephus's histories. But the story has Jesus working in the countryside in the different areas of Israelite heritage. This is implicit with regard to the Samaritans and the Galileans and the people on the other side of the Sea of Galilee (4:4-5, 39-41, 43-45; 6:1-14) and explicit "in the Judean countryside, . . . [where] he was baptizing more than John" (3:22-26). The story also locates key episodes and incidents in particular villages, with Cana and Capernaum prominent in Galilee and the village of Bethany near Jerusalem especially prominent in Judea (chs. 10–11). The story calls Sychar in Samaria a "city," but surely thinks of it as a large village, not a ruling city like Jerusalem or Sepphoris, since the earlier (Hasmonean) Judean high priesthood had destroyed the previous capital city of Samaria nearby.

John also has Jesus working among some of the ordinary people of Jerusalem (such as the people he heals on the Sabbath) who come to trust in him. But the story is clear that even the crowds in Jerusalem who respond to Jesus include (primarily) people from the countryside who have gone up to Jerusalem for one or another of the festivals of the Judeans (John 4:45; 11:55; 12:12; and probably 7:31).

The high priests, led by the presiding high priest Caiaphas, are clearly the rulers of the Judeans in the Gospel of John. Josephus states explicitly that, in Greco-Roman terms, Judeans were ruled by an aristocracy (*Antiquities* 20.251; cf. 11.111). Both Josephus and later rabbinic references indicate that this aristocracy consisted mainly of the four high priestly families that had been elevated by Herod as instruments of his rule (e.g., *Antiquities* 20.224-51; *War* 4.148-53; *bPesahim* 57a). This priestly aristocracy that ruled the temple-state was headed by the key high priestly officers, in turn headed by *the* high priest, who was appointed to the office by the current Roman governor. Josephus also indicates that leading scribes and Pharisees were among "the most prominent" or "the rulers" of Judea. With some variation of terminology, the Gospel of John, like the other Gospels, portrays the same set of figures as the rulers of the Judeans. It is clear from the narrative of Jesus' hearing before the high priest(s) and Pilate at the climax of the Gospel of John that the high priests are the heads of the temple-state. John's Gospel also refers to the Pharisees as "rulers," and (as mentioned above) refers to them along with the high priests as "the Judeans" in charge of affairs in Jerusalem and as the principal opponents of Jesus. John's "high priests and Pharisees/ Judeans" thus may be more or less the equivalent of the Synoptic Gospels' "high priests, elders, and scribes."

John's representation of the rulers bears particular resemblance to that of Josephus on just how dependent the high priests were on the Romans, whether the governor or the emperor. It is striking in Josephus's accounts that, despite the abuses of the people by the Roman governors and protests by the people, the high priests never seem to represent the interests of the people to the Romans. Rather, they invariably side with Rome in the conflicts that erupt, usually touched off by Roman provocations.[2] Josephus makes clear again and again that the high priests were instruments of the Roman imperial order, held responsible by the Romans to maintain control in Judea and to gather and deliver the tribute in timely fashion. The high priests were particularly vulnerable to the

2. See Richard Horsley, "The High Priests and the Politics of Roman Palestine: A Contextual Analysis of the Evidence in Josephus," *Journal for the Study of Judaism* 17 (1986), 23-55; Martin Goodman, *The Ruling Class of Judaea: The Origins of the Jewish Revolt against Rome, A.D. 66-70* (Cambridge: Cambridge University Press, 1987).

Roman governor, who appointed and demoted individual priests and also kept the priestly vestments under custody in the Antonia fortress, although the political dynamics of this relationship of course involved negotiation and mutual manipulation. That Caiaphas continued for years as high priest under the oversight of Pontius Pilate suggests that the two collaborated closely in the rule of Judea. In John's story, the portrayal of the high priests before Pilate is almost mocking: they appear as little more than sycophants, insisting that "everyone who claims to be a king (i.e., Jesus) sets himself against Caesar" while they themselves "have no king but Caesar" (John 19:12, 15).

In contrast to Pilate's reluctance to condemn Jesus in the Gospel of Matthew, John's portrayal of Pilate is a closer match for Josephus's accounts of the governor as aggressive in his treatment of the Judeans. In Josephus, Pilate is quick to send out the military to attack the movement led by the Samaritan prophet at Mount Gerizim (*Antiquities* 18.87). Earlier, shortly after he was appointed governor, Pilate had caused a major provocation of Judeans by sending his soldiers into Jerusalem under cover of night carrying their army standards, which bore symbols offensive to Judean laws (*War* 2.169-74; *Antiquities* 18.55-59). When the Judeans mounted a large nonviolent demonstration, literally "laying their bodies on the line" and daring Pilate to massacre them, however, he backed away from violently suppressing the protest. Later on, however, he did not hesitate to attack and slaughter Judeans who protested his use of funds from the sacred treasury of the temple to construct an aqueduct for Jerusalem (*War* 2.175-77; *Antiquities* 18.60-62). Acting in a similarly repressive manner, John's Pilate interrogates Jesus, tortures him, publicly mocks him, and then has him crucified after declaring him "innocent" several times. Pilate's insistence that he finds "no case against" Jesus and his efforts to release Jesus (John 18:38; 19:12) are clearly attempts to embarrass the priests in front of their own people, with his ultimate concession to their demands simply illustrating what will become of any aspiring "king of the Judeans."

John also resembles Josephus's accounts with regard to the Jerusalem high priests not having authority from the Romans to carry out execution (John 18:31). Perhaps the most poignant illustration of this rule is the high priest Ananus, who was deposed for ordering the execution of

James, the brother of Jesus, in the early 60s (*Antiquities* 20.200-203). While the outcomes of the stories are different, John's portrayal of the high priests' arrest of Jesus and handing him over to the governor corresponds to their handling of the prophet Jesus son of Hananiah some thirty years later during the governorship of Albinus (*War* 6.300-309). In Josephus's account of that incident, the high priests ("the most prominent figures of the city"/"the rulers") apprehend a prophetic figure they find threatening to the Roman imperial order, then hand him over to the Roman governor for punishment or execution. Judging this Jesus to be mad, Albinus has him released after torture.

In this connection, recent translations of the Gospel of John have used somewhat misleading terminology in their descriptions of the men sent to arrest Jesus (7:32, 45; 18:12). The New Revised Standard Version refers to them as "the temple police" and "the Jewish police," while the New Jerusalem Bible calls them "the temple guards" and "the Jewish guards" — in both cases the word "Jewish" apparently distinguishing them from Roman soldiers. The words "police" and "guards," however, may suggest an official standing and legitimacy that these individuals do not possess in John's story, or even that John would not attribute to the means by which the high priests maintained "public order." The Greek text simply says that "the high priests and the Pharisees sent servants *(hypēretai)*" to get Jesus (7:32, 45-46), and that "the servants *(hoi hypēretai)* of the Judeans" (= the high priests and Pharisees), along with "the soldiers and their officers" (18:12), finally arrested him. It should be kept in mind, in assessing who these "servants" of the high priests and the Pharisees may be, that in Judea at the time leading high priestly figures deployed their own gangs of "servants" (*douloi, oiketai;* "strong men," "thugs," *Antiquities* 20.181, 206-7), who Josephus says functioned as "enforcers" for the high priests.

With regard to the "retainers," the scribes and Pharisees who served as advisers and representatives of the priestly aristocracy that controlled the temple-state, John's portrayal again fits the reconstruction on the basis of references in Josephus sketched in chapter 1 above. The Pharisees clearly operated as prominent and influential figures in the Hasmonean regime. While they played at least a subordinate role at Herod's court, they evidently returned to a more significant role in the high priestly regime under the oversight of the Roman governors. We cannot otherwise explain how "the leading Pharisees" could have emerged to such prominence in the "provisional government" that attempted to exert minimal control over Judea and Galilee after the Romans were driven out in the early excitement of the great revolt in the summer of 66 CE.

The Gospel of John shows them in a similarly prominent role, working side by side with the high priests in attempts to maintain public order, at least in Jerusalem itself, especially as interpreters and enforcers of the Law of Moses. In this regard, John, like Matthew, gives the Pharisees a more prominent role in the operation of the temple-state than does Mark, who shows (some of) the scribes side by side with the high priests. John also has the Pharisees operating (only) in Jerusalem itself, similar to what is suggested in Josephus's accounts, whereas Mark's story (followed by Matthew and Luke) has them coming to Galilee to dispute with Jesus. But Galilee was not under Jerusalem jurisdiction during the lifetime of Jesus. In Josephus's accounts only in the turmoil during the revolt in 66-67 CE are a few Pharisees included in a delegation sent to Galilee by the provisional high priestly regime in Jerusalem. Otherwise they operate in Jerusalem, exactly where John locates their conflicts with Jesus.

John's representation of the dynamics between the rulers in Jerusalem and the people in and from the villages also mirrors what is evident in Josephus's accounts. As mentioned in chapter 1, Josephus discusses several movements based in the countryside headed by popular prophets or populist kings that were sufficiently threatening to the established order to provoke the rulers (mainly the Romans) to take action to suppress them. Josephus also portrays the Passover festival in Jerusalem as the occasion of a number of popular outcries against the rulers. Similarly, in John the Passover and other festivals are occasions of protest, but John of course focuses on Jesus as the main spokesperson or actor, rallying the people who have come up for the festivals. There are some interesting resemblances between John's portrayal of Jesus' accusations and protests against the high priests and Pharisees and what they represent and the people's protests against the oppressive practices of Herod and his high priests in 4 BCE, as Archelaus was attempting to take over Judea just after his father's death (*War* 2.4-7; *Antiquities* 17.204-7).[3]

---

3. For comparative analysis of protests of the urban crowd in Jerusalem, see Rich-

John's presentation of Jesus' mission thus fits the historical context quite well in terms of the main social-political division and dynamics, in some ways more fully than does Mark's. It would be difficult in the extreme, of course, to know and verify particulars, such as whether a prophet from the countryside would repeatedly engage in heated argument with high priests and Pharisees. Certainly, when such figures were apprehended they were interrogated, as in the case of Jesus son of Hananiah. Of course, if a popular prophet made a persistent nuisance of himself, the high priests would take notice and perhaps take action. A teacher or prophet, moreover, could easily draw a small crowd somewhere in the milling crowd in the temple courtyard, and representatives of the rulers might well take notice.

Galileans, Samaritans, and Judeans

John's story also parallels contemporary Judean sources such as Josephus in making clear regional distinctions between "Galilee/the Galileans," "Samaria/the Samaritans," and "Judea/the Judeans." The Gospel of Mark also assumes these regional distinctions, although this has usually been overlooked, perhaps because, except for the title on the cross, Mark makes only one clear reference to "the Judeans," and there only in referring to purity customs that are advocated by the Jerusalem Pharisees and scribes who have come to Galilee to challenge Jesus (Mark 7:1-7). Of course, the distinctions among regions of Israelites has been obscured in reading of John's Gospel as well, insofar as the concepts "Judaism" and "Christianity" have been imposed on the story, with the translation of *hoi Ioudaioi* as "the Jews" having tragic effects.

John's story, however, could not be clearer about the different regions, and in fact amplifies the distinctions by the very fact of having Jesus move regularly between and within all of them. The narrative clearly and repeatedly indicates Jesus' movement from one region to another, and is even clear about the geographical relation of the regions: "he left Judea

---

ard Horsley, *Jesus and the Spiral of Violence: Popular Resistance in Roman Palestine* (San Francisco: Harper & Row, 1987), 90-99.

and started back to Galilee. But he had to go through Samaria.... He went from that place to Galilee" (4:3-4, 43). John also mentions the people of each area explicitly, sometimes in distinction to people of other regions. "Many Samaritans . . . trusted in him . . . the Samaritans came to him" (4:39-40), after which, "when he came to Galilee, the Galileans welcomed him, since they had seen all that he had done in Jerusalem" (where he had confronted "the Judeans," that is, the rulers; v. 45). John clearly portrays "the Judeans'" (the Pharisees' and rulers') disdain for Galilee and Galileans (7:51-52). The continuing conflict between Samaritans and Judeans could not be clearer in John and is stated not in vague ethnic terms but rather in terms of the central dispute between them regarding the proper place of worship (4:7-20). John's portrayal of these mutual hostilities between the people of the different regions again parallels that in Josephus's histories, as illustrated, for example, in the two major incidents of the bones strewn in the temple and the attacks and counterattacks of Samaritans and Judeans under the governor Cumanus, discussed earlier in chapter 2.

While Mark implies that Jesus himself is a Galilean, John makes this explicit: Galilee is his *patris* (4:43-44).[4] The discussion between the Samaritan woman and Jesus might cause some confusion for interpreters in this regard, particularly since the woman refers to him as a "Judean" (v. 9), an assertion that Jesus does not deny. The larger context and movement of the dialogue, however, are critical: Jesus has just arrived in Sychar from Judea not long after a Passover festival, so the woman naturally assumes that he is a Judean. Jesus plays along with her assumption, stating among other things that "salvation is from the Judeans" (v. 22) in specific contrast to Samaritan religious practices. By the conclusion of the discussion, however, she recognizes that Jesus is the Messiah and "the Savior of the world," and that "salvation" is through him, not through the Judeans or the temple in Jerusalem. Jesus' clear statement that true worship of God is in no way confined to or even centralized in

---

4. On the meaning of the "prophet without honor" saying in John, see Gilbert Van Belle, "The Faith of the Galileans," *Ephemerides theologicae lovanienses* 74 (1998), 27-44, and "The Prophetic Power of the Word of Jesus: A Study of John 4,43-54," in *Prophecy, Wisdom, and Spirit in the Johannine Literature*, ed. B. Decharneux and F. Nobilio (Brussels: EME, 2013).

the Jerusalem temple is consistent with John's overall portrayal of Jesus, the prophet/messiah from Galilee, in conflict with "the Judeans," that is, the Jerusalem rulers. In John, the Pharisees and high priests view Jesus and his followers as Galileans involved in a movement that originated in Galilee (7:51-52), and "the Judeans" insult him by referring to him as a "Samaritan" (8:48), the basic point being "he's not one of us."

John's story also shows Jesus traveling into the Transjordan and to the other side of the Sea of Galilee (6:1-14; 10:40-42). The latter appears to refer to the area north of the Decapolis that was assigned to Herod Philip. In John's Gospel Andrew, Peter, and Philip (and Nathanael?) are all from Bethsaida (1:44-45), a village just across the Jordan River not far from Capernaum that Herod Philip had raised to the status of a "city" as one of his residences (Josephus, *Antiquities* 18.28). Various references in Josephus and other sources offer two possibilities for understanding Jesus' work "across the Jordan" (10:40-42). One is Perea, the larger area east of the Jordan and south of the Sea of Galilee that was, like Galilee, under the rule of Herod Antipas. The note that Jesus returned to "the place where John had been baptizing earlier," "Bethany across the Jordan" (1:28), suggests another possibility. *Bethania* appears without the article in John 1:28, and "the place" in 10:40 may refer to an indefinite area, not a particular village. It thus seems quite possible that *Bethania* could refer to Batanea, the area across the Jordan just east and south of the Sea of Galilee. This would have been an obvious area to which Jesus could retreat from the Judeans simply because it was ruled by Herod Philip, whom Josephus describes as moderate and easy-going in his rule. It was also an area of Israelite heritage. Josephus explains that "many people devoted to the ancestral customs of the Judeans" had settled there during Herod's reign (*Antiquities* 17.23-27).

The Gospel of John also gives a few indications of the particular political-cultural dynamics of the historical relations between Galileans and their rulers. Although John makes no mention of Herod's son Antipas, whom the Romans appointed as tetrarch (ruler of a quarter of his father's kingdom) during the lifetime of Jesus, the reference to "the royal official" whose son lay sick in Capernaum evidently accords with the Galilean popular understanding of Antipas as "king" (John 4:46-54). Josephus refers to Antipas by his official title in reference to the palace he built in his second capital, Tiberias (*Life* 65), but Antipas was popularly known as "king," like his father, and his officers called "royal." Even though he had been raised at the imperial court in Rome, he probably brought into his administration Judeans with some experience in his father's regime in Jerusalem or already deployed as "Herodian" officers in Galilee. Thus, it is possible that "the royal officer" who comes to Jesus in Cana seeking help for his child is a Judean, not a "Gentile."[5]

It might seem strange, once we recognize John's clear distinctions among the different regions, that there are water jars "for the purification rites of the Judeans" in Cana, a village in Galilee. But of course, as illustrated by the "royal officer" of Antipas, there were Judeans resident in Galilee and had been for several generations after the Hasmoneans took control of the region a hundred years before Jesus' birth. The Hasmoneans and then Herod maintained garrisoned fortresses in the area to maintain order and security and to collect taxes. Josephus mentions Sepphoris, Gabara, and Yodfat as prominent towns in Galilee, reflecting their history as administrative sites. That Cana was an important village in Galilee is indicated by the fact that Josephus himself made the town his headquarters for a time when he was trying to hold the Galileans in check as an appointee of the provisional high priestly regime during the revolt in 66-67 CE (*Life* 86). And it would have been just such "ranking" Judeans as the officers of such administrative towns who would have been concerned to maintain ritual purity, in contrast with Galilean peasants who lived in the towns and villages overseen by those officers. The latter, remote from and relatively unacquainted with the purity codes of life in Jerusalem, would likely have viewed such ritual purity as unimportant in/for their local community life.

The village of Bethany, only two miles from Jerusalem on the slope of the Mount of Olives, plays an important role in John's plot, even more than in Mark's story. In Mark, Bethany is the village from which Jesus stages his entry into Jerusalem, sending two of his disciples to get the donkey (evidently by prearrangement), and to which he then withdraws

---

5. Not even Matthew's version of the story (8:5-13), read in the context of the whole story in which Jesus twice instructs his disciples to "go only to the lost sheep of the house of Israel" (10:6; 15:24), suggests that the "centurion" is a Gentile, but rather an officer of Antipas.

with his disciples after his forcible demonstration in the temple (Mark 11:1-3, 11). In John, Bethany is the village of Mary and Martha and their brother Lazarus, whom Jesus raises, leading "many Judeans" to become loyal to him and making his movement seriously threatening to the high priests and Pharisees (John 11:1-48; 12:11). One of the factors that led to this expansion of his movement was the "many Judeans" who had come to offer consolation for the death of Lazarus and then responded with trust when Jesus raised him. Bethany is the point from which Jesus proceeds up to Jerusalem acclaimed as the populist king of Israel (12:1, 9-19).

What is known from various sources about the considerable expansion of Jerusalem and massive reconstruction of the temple, particularly under Herod, with the attendant impact on nearby villages, may help to explain why and how Bethany and its people might play such a role in Jesus' movement. Prior to the Maccabean Revolt, Jerusalem was a relatively small city, capital of the relatively limited area of Judea. But the Hasmonean dynasty, which consolidated its power in the aftermath of the revolt, expanded the territory it ruled through the conquests of Idumea and Samaria and the takeover of Galilee, with an attendant expansion of Jerusalem. Herod's massive reconstruction of the temple mount as the monumental religious-political-economic center for Jews of the Diaspora as well as his own subjects brought further expansion of the city, which now attracted many Diaspora Jews as pilgrims (such as Saul of Tarsus and "the Greeks" who ask Philip if they can see Jesus in John 12:20-21). Such expansion would have displaced some residents in villages such as Bethany, while they or others would have found work in the construction of the temple complex. In the intensified contact and coming and going between village and city, the resulting communication between them would have provided "intelligence" about what was happening in the city and contacts inside. Bethany also would have provided a potential base of operations for a prophet from the countryside to enter the city under the protection of crowds during festival days, and a place to which he could retreat for safety.

The Cultural Divide

The Gospel of John offers a number of indications that Jesus and his movement of loyalists were speaking and acting from the popular Israelite tradition vis-à-vis the official Jerusalem tradition. One clue to the orientation of
John's story is that the various debates about Jesus' identity in the narrative seem to represent the viewpoints of the ordinary people, not that of
the high priestly rulers and Pharisees (e.g., 7:12-13, 25-27, 40-43; 10:19-20).

As summarized earlier in chapter 1, Judean sources offer evidence of
a different version of Israelite tradition operative among the people from
the official tradition now familiar from the extant Judean texts, some of
which were later included in the Hebrew Bible. Judean texts from late
second temple times, for example, rarely refer to a "messiah" who will
lead the restoration of Israel in resistance to the imperial rulers, and
most of these references appear in texts produced by dissident scribal
circles (e.g., *Psalms of Solomon* 17 and a few texts from Qumran). As noted
above, however, Josephus offers evidence of several concrete messianic
movements among the people in which they acclaimed their leaders
"kings," working from the vivid popular memory of the young David being "anointed" by ancient Israelites to fight oppressive invaders. While it
seems clear from recent research on orality and literacy and text-critical
research that direct knowledge of the books of Torah was limited to scribal circles associated with the temple, Josephus gives examples of Galilean villagers taking action against their rulers in defense of one or another of the basic commandments of the Mosaic covenant. Josephus also
indicates that the people occasionally agitated against their rulers at the
official celebration of the Passover in the temple under the demeaning
oversight of Roman soldiers (as discussed in chapter 1).

Again, the Gospel of John fits just this cultural divide between the
high priestly rulers and scribal circles (Pharisees), on the one hand, and
the ordinary people, on the other. Most telling, perhaps, is John's regular
identification of the elaborate festivals held in the Jerusalem temple as
"of the Judeans" — that is, as operated by the high priests and Pharisees.
In John's story, if not in the history of its interpretation, this is not simply
a matter of a "Christian" dis-identification with "Judaism" — of which
there is no suggestion whatsoever in the Fourth Gospel — but rather a

reflection of the divide between the rulers and the ruled, between the officials in Jerusalem and the villagers in the countryside, as compounded by the regional differences of the Galileans and Samaritan villagers who had only recently been brought under Jerusalem rule. A clear indication of this cultural divide appears in John's juxtaposition of a story in which "the Judeans" decree that anyone who confesses Jesus as the Messiah will be expelled from (the assembly of) the people (9:18-23) with Jesus' argument about "the sheepfold," that is, membership in the people, and his own role as the shepherd who gives his life for the sheep (10:1-30), all set during the festival of Booths (7:2) and immediately before another incident during the festival of the Dedication (10:22-30).

Key episodes in John's story may well reflect rival or contested claims to key figures and events in Israelite tradition by the Jerusalem elite, on the one hand, and ordinary Israelites, on the other. The "Judeans'" claim to be "descendants of Abraham" and Jesus' refutation and counterclaim that he fulfills and supersedes (the heritage of) Abraham appears to be a prime example of such a contest (John 8:31-59). In the Synoptics, John the Baptist's declaration that "God can raise up children to Abraham from these stones" (Q/Luke 3:7-9), in Matthew specifically directed to the Pharisees and Sadducees (3:7-10), appears to reflect the same contest over Abraham as the great ancestor and progenitor of Israel. As suggested in both John and Matthew, it was particularly important to the Jerusalem elite, whose legitimacy as rulers was in serious question among dissident retainers, ordinary Jerusalemites, and villagers alike,[6] to claim ancestry in the patriarchs and matriarchs, particularly Abraham. A prime example was Herod, an Idumean military strongman who had been appointed king by the Romans and then conquered his own subjects. Among his various strategies of obtaining legitimacy, Herod constructed a huge monument over the caves of Machpelah near Hebron, which Abraham had bought for a family burial site (Gen 23:1-20; 25:9; 49:30; 50:13; Num 13:22), and then established religious observances at his new shrine.[7]

---

6. See Goodman, *Ruling Class;* Richard Horsley, *Revolt of the Scribes: Resistance and Apocalyptic Origins* (Minneapolis: Fortress, 2010), especially chapters 4 and 6-10.

7. See Peter Richardson, *Herod: King of the Jews and Friend of the Romans* (Columbia: University of South Carolina Press, 1996), 60-61, with additional references.

In John's story the cultural divide is evident especially with regard to "the law." This is particularly striking once we reject the old division between "Judaism" and nascent "Christianity" that was imposed on the Gospel but is simply not evident in the text. The high priests and Pharisees disdain the crowd as accursed because they "do not know the law" (7:49) and they, "the Judeans," look down upon Jesus because he has not had scribal training (v. 15). They know from their Scripture that the Messiah will come from Bethlehem in Judea, not from Galilee, and that "no prophet is to arise from Galilee" (vv. 42, 52).

Similar to the ambivalence of ordinary people to writing in general and the ambivalence of ordinary Judeans and Galileans to the sacred scrolls of the temple-state in Jerusalem, the Gospel of John displays an ambivalence to the "law" or "Scripture" of "the Judeans." This ambivalent attitude toward the law is evident in the simple terms of reference. Parallel to the Roman governor Pilate's distancing reference to it as "your law" (18:31), Jesus himself refers to the law as "your law" in addressing "the Judeans" and "their law" in addressing the disciples (7:19; 15:25). The high priests, on the other hand, proudly claim it: "we have a law . . ." (19:7). John presents Jesus as standing over against the law as something that belongs to the Judean high priests and Pharisees and as sharply critical of both the law and the Judeans' use of it. Yet the Gospel also recognizes the authority of the law and the Scripture generally and insists that Jesus fulfils the law in significant ways.

John's recognition of the authority of the law/Scripture reflects the relation of ordinary Judeans and Galileans to the sacred scrolls of the temple-state in two principal ways. The people of Judea and Galilee, including Jesus and his loyalists and the composers of John's story, knew that the contents of the Judeans' law/Scripture were in significant respects the same as or parallel to the popular tradition in which they were rooted and out of which they were speaking. Precisely in their opposition to the temple-state, therefore, they could appeal to particular contents of the Scripture/law against the rulers who appealed to it for their own legitimation. In a largely non-literate society, moreover, the Scripture/law held a special authority simply because it stood written. Accordingly, at several points the Gospel of John cites a phrase or general reference from "the Scripture" either in specific opposition to those who claim to possess it, or to claim the high authority of the official Judean Scripture for Jesus (5:45-46; 7:38, 42; 13:18; 17:12, etc.). Even then, it fits the oral orientation of the people that, while Moses and the prophets are understood as having been (or being) "written," "the writing" (Scripture) itself is understood as having "spoken" (7:38, 42).

On the other hand, while John and John's Jesus appeal to the authority of the Scripture, the law (of the Judeans) is an object of conflict, is contested. Jesus is not only from the remote district of Galilee, which (in the view of the high priests and Pharisees) could not possibly produce a prophet and certainly could not be the provenance of a messiah. He is also utterly uneducated, that is, he has not properly learned the (official) cultural traditions, including the law according to which the temple-state is operated (7:14-15). Yet he goes on the attack. And in the episodes in which the law figures in the conflict, Jesus knows Israelite tradition in sufficient detail to confute the official guardians in their inconsistency.

"Did not Moses give *you* the law?" His rhetorical question redirects their claim to possess the law given them by Moses back against them. They claim to have been given the law by Moses. But they do not keep it (7:19-24). In this case he attacks their inconsistent application of the law to justify his healing on the Sabbath. They hold that circumcision has such high importance that they will violate Sabbath laws in order to circumcise by a certain time/age, yet they will not allow the healing of a man's whole body. After he has done another healing, of a blind man, as the Judeans are about to stone him for claiming to be God's Son in doing his Father's works, Jesus again challenges them with a line from "their" own law and their own principle of its inviolability. "Is it not written in your law . . . ," and, of course, "the Scripture cannot be annulled" (10:31-36). As illustrated in these episodes, John's Jesus sharply contests the law as something the rulers use to justify their control of the people. Not only is Jesus not particularly concerned to be obeying the law, but he rejects its application as a hindrance to his bringing healing and life to the people.

The Historical Johannine Jesus

CHAPTER SEVEN

John's Jesus and the Renewal of Israel

Building on the steps taken in earlier chapters, we now examine more fully and carefully the portrayal of Jesus in the Gospel of John. The summary of the Gospel's narrative in chapter 5 provided an overview of John's story of Jesus. In chapter 6 we noted the significant ways in which the fourth Gospel's story "fits" the historical situation in early Roman Palestine, particularly with regard to the fundamental divisions between the ordinary people and their rulers and among the different regions of Israelite heritage, as sketched in chapters 1 and 2. Now we are ready to explore the main agenda of Jesus' mission as presented in John, our principal purpose and focus in this book. This will also be a necessary step before attempting to use the Gospel as a source for the historical Jesus.

Just as the plot of the Gospel story is not the same as an outline, so the Gospel's portrayal of the mission of Jesus is more than its plot, though it is discerned only in the overall literary context of the Gospel's plot, setting, and characters. Prominent features of the main plot may be important indicators. But seemingly less important episodes or what appear almost as "tags" to some of the main events of the story may also be important indicators of Jesus' main agenda according to the Gospel of John. And just as the plot of the Gospel can be appreciated only by reading the story in its ancient historical context, so the Gospel's portrayal of Jesus' mission can be appreciated only with considerable attention to the historical context.

The portrayal of Jesus and his mission in John, like that in Mark and the other Synoptic Gospels, is strikingly different from the interpretations of Jesus based in the standard Christian theological scheme of Christian origins. According to this scheme of how the new religion, Christianity, originated in and split off from the old religion Judaism, Jesus is the great individual revealer but not the leader of a movement. The latter, which became the church, was founded only after his resurrection by his disciples. This scheme involves a projection of the later synthetic constructs of "Judaism" and "Christianity" onto the Gospels and other texts. Interpreters working within the scheme often cite Acts 2:46 as evidence that Jesus' disciples were still faithfully worshiping in the Jewish Temple, as suggested by the King James Version and even the Revised Standard Version: "day by day attending the temple." The New Revised Standard Version has clarified the situation: they were "spending time in the temple [courtyard]," which was the only public space where they might be recruiting. The standard scheme of Christian origins simply abstracts Jesus from the fundamental social forms, communication, and social interaction of his own time. This scheme still influences the way interpreters understand Jesus in the Gospels, especially in the Gospel of John, as well as much interpretation of the historical Jesus.

Once the Gospel of John is read as a whole story, however, then, like the Synoptic Gospels, it can be seen to portray Jesus in interaction with followers and opponents in the fundamental social forms and dynamics of the historical context. In contrast to the standard scheme of Christian origins, in fact, John and the other Gospels portray Jesus as catalyzing a movement in opposition to the Jerusalem rulers and their Roman patrons. And, far from a revealer of teaching that forms the basis of a new religion, "(early) Christianity," in opposition to "(early) Judaism," Jesus is portrayed in John, as well as in Mark, Q, and Matthew, as engaged in the renewal of Israel. This can be discerned in the acts he performs as signs and in his working in all the regions of Israelite heritage. It is then confirmed in the many ways that John portrays Jesus as the fulfillment of Israelite tradition, particularly in the roles in which his followers acclaim him and in the roles that he fills in his renewal of the people in opposition to the rulers.

Generating a Movement

While John's story focuses on Jesus himself, it portrays Jesus, accompanied and assisted by his disciples, as generating a growing *movement* of people. In fact, John makes the development of a movement of followers more explicit than it is in Mark's story and the Q speeches. Mark presents ever widening circles hearing about and responding to Jesus' teaching and healings and exorcism. As in John, large crowds eagerly hear him and eventually acclaim him on his entry into Jerusalem. That this response has become a movement, however, is more implicit in Mark and Q, evident mainly in particular components of those texts, such as Jesus' speeches of instruction for community life (Mark 10:2-45; Q/Luke 6:20-49) and admonition to maintain solidarity under repression (Mark 8:34-38; Q/Luke 12:2-12). By contrast, John presents Jesus quite explicitly generating a movement in the repeated references to many people who, having seen the signs, become loyal to Jesus.

The significance of the response to Jesus may not seem evident at first in the response to the first sign of water into wine at the wedding in Cana, where John mentions only that "the disciples trusted in him" (2:1-11). But it quickly becomes clear when, in response to his baptizing in the countryside of Judea, "all [were] going to him," so that the Pharisees had heard that "Jesus is making and baptizing more disciples than John" (3:22, 26; 4:1). Then the movement expands in Samaria, where in response to his teaching "many Samaritans came to trust in him" and "many more trusted in his word" (4:39, 41). The movement appears to expand dramatically in Galilee in response to the signs of his healings and the sign of the mass feeding, as the people acclaim him as the prophet and prepare to make him king (6:1-15). In stating that the Judean rulers had agreed that anyone who confessed Jesus to be the Messiah would be "expelled from the assembly" (of the people), the narrative suggests that the movement had been growing steadily, such that it was now a threat to the rulers (9:22). In a brief account John also makes a point of the movement's expansion into the area "across the Jordan," where, again, "many came to him . . . and many became loyal to him" (10:40-42). The high priests and Pharisees finally planned to take action against him after "many of the Judeans . . . became loyal to him" after the raising of Lazarus (11:45-48), and their concerns were confirmed by the "great crowd of Judeans" who acclaimed his entry into Jerusalem.

John's story, moreover, portrays a movement that has a kind of infrastructure of leadership in the form of the disciples. While John has no equivalent of the commissioning of twelve disciples in Mark and Q, "the disciples," those who first come to trust in Jesus (2:11), appear repeatedly in the story as a kind of inner circle who accompany Jesus from place to place, assisting and questioning him (2:12; 3:22; 6:3, 12-13; 11:7-12, 54). John also uses the term in reference to a wider circle of Jesus-loyalists who respond to his mission (4:1; 6:60-66; 8:31; 9:27-28; 15:8). The Gospel gives the impression at key points in the story, however, that within the wider circle is an inner circle of disciples who are more or less the same as "the Twelve." When many of Jesus' disciples find it difficult to accept that "the bread of life" is his own flesh and body and "turn back," the Twelve persist in their loyalty (6:66-70). In any case, an inner circle of disciples, including the Twelve, continues to travel with him, retreating with him to the wilderness to avoid arrest (11:54). They are with him at the supper at which he delivers the long discourse about love and the Spirit and are the disciples to whom the resurrected Jesus appears, Thomas being "one of the Twelve" (13:5, 22-23; 20:19-29). In addition to the inner circle of disciples, particular followers that John mentions by name appear to hold important leadership roles, perhaps in the different regions — for example, Nathanael in Bethsaida and Mary, Martha, and Lazarus in Bethany. Thus, while John's story portrays Jesus primarily as a revealer who almost transcends the world of every day, he also represents Jesus as leading a growing movement that has a certain infrastructure.

In the context of the Roman Empire and in Israelite tradition, *pistis/ fides* — "trust (in)" or "loyalty (to)," but usually translated as "faith" or "belief" — meant loyalty to a particular overlord or leader and not to another. Subject people were expected to be "faithful"/loyal to Rome and Caesar. In Israelite tradition, "faith" or "trust" had a similar meaning: the Israelites were to trust in and remain loyal to God as their exclusive Lord and Master, as articulated in the first two commandments of the Mosaic covenant. In the Roman imperial order, loyalty might well involve a hierarchy, as when Herod required that his subjects take an oath of loyalty to both himself and Rome/Caesar. This oath created an acute conflict for those committed to the Mosaic covenantal demand of exclusive loyalty to God. Interestingly, according to Josephus, the Pharisees, some of the professional retainers responsible for the cultivation of Mosaic covenantal law, refused to submit to the oath (*Antiquities* 17.42). More radical Pharisees such as Saddok and the teacher Judas from Gamala even organized resistance to payment of tribute, apparently on the grounds that it would compromise exclusive loyalty to God as Lord and Master (*Antiquities* 18.4-5, 23-25).

The implications in John's story are that the people who became loyal to Jesus were withdrawing their loyalty to the high priestly rulers and, by implication, the Roman imperial order they represented. This is clearly signaled when the Judean rulers decide that anyone loyal to Jesus be "expelled from the assembly" (of the people) over whom they presumed to preside (9:22). John presents this most dramatically as well as most explicitly in the high priestly recognition that if Jesus is allowed to continue his work, then "everyone will become loyal to him and the Romans will come and destroy our holy place and our people" (11:47-48). The movement that is building is by clear implication also a movement of resistance to the temple-state in Jerusalem and the Roman imperial order it represents.

The Renewal of Israel

The Gospel of John repeatedly represents Jesus as engaged in the renewal of Israel. Jesus' feeding of the crowd on the mountain "across the Sea of Galilee" is particularly rich in such symbolism. Jesus enacts the feeding as a new Moses, and in the ensuing discussion embodies the bread of life, prefigured in the manna, the bread from heaven (6:1-34). Not surprisingly, the people recognize him as the prophet who is to come (v. 14). John has the disciples "gather" or "assemble" *(synagagein)* the remains of the feast into twelve baskets, clearly representing the twelve tribes of Israel (vv. 12-13). Just as in the "twelve" commissioned to extend Jesus' mission in Mark and the "twelve" on "twelve" seats dispensing justice for the people in the Q speech, "the Twelve" in John are representative of Israel undergoing renewal. And Jesus' admonition to the disciples that "the fields are ripe for the harvesting" and that they are being sent to reap — among the Samaritan villagers, no less — appears to be John's allusive parallel to the more explicit commissioning speeches in the Synoptics (4:31-38). Most of the signs that Jesus performs signal the renewal of the people of Israel. Two provide abundant food or drink (2:1-11; 6:1-13), two provide new life from debilitating disease, despite one's sins, and the raising of Lazarus embodies as well as symbolizes "the resurrection and life" of the body-politic. The healing of the royal official's son at a distance and the raising of Lazarus, moreover, recall the actions of Elijah and Elisha, archetypal prophets of renewal (cf. 1 Kgs 17:17-24; 2 Kgs 4:18-37; 5:9-14).

Surely most striking — and unique to the Gospel of John — is that Jesus works and generates a movement of renewal in all the regions of Israelite heritage. Mark and, to a lesser degree, Q show Jesus engaged in a renewal of Israel in some but not all Israelite regions. The place names in the Q speeches seem to envision Jesus working mainly in Galilee, while Mark also shows him acting beyond the frontiers of Galilee in the villages of Tyre, Caesarea Philippi, and the Decapolis. In Mark, Jesus does eventually move through "the region of Judea and beyond the Jordan," then delivers important teaching in Judea, and leaves Jericho for Jerusalem with a large crowd. John, by contrast, shows Jesus regularly moving back and forth between Galilee, Judea, Samaria, and the region across the Jordan, building a following among the villagers of each region. By having Jesus active in all the regions where Israelite villagers were located, John signals that the purpose of Jesus' mission was a renewal of Israel and not simply a declaration of transcendent truths symbolized by miraculous signs.

John indicates clearly that Galilee was Jesus's *patris,* his "native country" (4:43-44). Jesus begins his mission in Galilee and spends time there, particularly in Capernaum, with his family, his disciples, and other responsive Galileans (1:43; 4:45). He does his first act designated as a "sign" in Cana of Galilee, using jars for the rites of purification of the Judeans in a way for which they were not intended, thus leading "his disciples to trust in him" (2:1-11). After Jesus' first southern tour, the Galileans "welcomed him, since they had seen all that he had done in Jerusalem" (4:45) — including apparently the attack on the temple and a number of unspecified signs (2:23-25; 3:2). Again in Cana, Jesus heals the child of a royal officer (by a simple declaration), leading the official and his whole household to place their trust in Jesus (as opposed to Antipas? 4:53). When Jesus returns to Capernaum following his feeding of the multitude on the mountain, the people eagerly beseech him to "give us this bread (of life)." Certainly not coincidentally, Jesus delivers the "living bread" near the time when the Judeans were celebrating Passover (6:4).

In all these episodes, it is impossible to miss the mutual regional hostility of the Galileans and the Judeans. The Galileans seem delighted at Jesus' attack on the temple and only too happy about the new wilderness feeding as a clear alternative to the official Passover festival in Jerusalem. The Judeans, both members of the crowd and the high priests and the Pharisees, identify Jesus and his mission as originating in and evidently originally based in Galilee among Galileans. But while recognizing that Galileans are included in "Israel," they look down on them. Despite the many signs Jesus performs, they dismiss him: nothing good can come from Galilee, surely not the Messiah or a prophet (7:41, 52).

Nevertheless, John portrays Jesus as working widely in Judea among Judeans, including not only the metropolis of Jerusalem but also the countryside villages, and states several times that "many Judeans placed their trust in Jesus." Jesus goes up to Jerusalem repeatedly, for three Passover festivals of the Judeans, for an unnamed festival, for the festival of Booths, and even for the festival of Dedication. John also has him spend time in the countryside of Judea, where he and/or his disciples were baptizing and generating a wide response (3:22). One suspects that John is making a summary generalization of the larger effects of Jesus' entire ministry after the demonstration in the temple with "when he was in Jerusalem during the Passover festival, many trusted in his name because they saw the signs that he was doing" (2:23). From the point of view of the rulers of the Judeans, the response to Jesus quickly reached alarming proportions. As the Baptist's disciples point out, "behold he is baptizing and all are going to him" (3:26). The Pharisees are concerned that "Jesus is making and baptizing more disciples than John" (4:1). Jesus' healings of the paralytic and the blind man in Jerusalem made a powerful impression on the crowd; the implication is that more than just the healed blind man became disciples (9:28; cf. 8:31: "the Judeans who had trusted in him").

In a brief account John also makes a point of having Jesus work in the area "across the Jordan" River, where John had been baptizing. As in the other traditional Israelite areas, "many came to him . . . and many trusted in him there" (10:40-42).

Most striking with regard to John portraying Jesus as engaged in a renewal of Israel is his encounter with the Samaritans (4:4-30, 39-42). As indicated in the narrative, there was intense mutual hostility between the Judeans and Samaritans. The woman at the well mistakes Jesus for a Judean and is surprised that he asks for a drink (from her vessel), since "Judeans do not share things in common with Samaritans." As the conversation proceeds, however, Jesus wins her over, and because of her testimony "many Samaritans . . . trusted in him" (vv. 39-42). In the previous conflicts between Judea and Samaria, and especially in the Jerusalem high priesthood's destruction of Shechem and the Samaritan temple nearby, Judeans and Samaritans had become hopelessly alienated, and Judeans had become cut off from some of the earlier cultural heritage of Israel. John presents Jesus reclaiming that heritage and including the Samaritans in Israel under renewal, focused in a discussion of how the issue of where to worship God will be transcended as people worship neither in Jerusalem nor on Gerizim, but in spirit and truth. John's pointed inclusion of the Samaritans in the renewal of the people of Israel stands in contrast with Matthew apparently excluding Samaritans from the renewal of Israel when Matthew's Jesus instructs the twelve not to enter Samaritan villages but to go "only to the lost sheep of the house of Israel" (Matt 10:5-6; cf. 15:21-24).[1]

John's portrayal of Jesus as working in the countryside or village communities in all the regions of Israelite heritage suggests that his agenda was the renewal of the people in a political-economic sense, not

1. The Gospel of Luke may be closer to John's inclusion of the Samaritans. On the one hand, Luke represents the acute tensions between the Samaritans and the Judeans (as represented by a "lawyer," 10:25-37) and even the disciples from Galilee (James and John, 9:51-56), and represents a Samaritan as a "stranger" (17:11-19). On the other hand, however, Luke has Jesus (a) rebuke the two disciples for wanting to call down fire from heaven against an inhospitable village (9:51-56), (b) use a Samaritan as an exemplar for how one should love one's neighbor (10:25-37), and (c) use a Samaritan leper as a paradigm of gratitude for healing and trust (17:11-19).

merely "spiritually" or symbolically. Mark's story and the Q speeches both have Jesus' mission focused on village communities. It is more striking that John's story, which focuses so heavily on Jesus' disputes with the Judean rulers in Jerusalem, also shows Jesus working in "the countryside" or in villages, which were the fundamental social form in which the people of Israel was constituted. John has Jesus not just passing through but "spending some time" or "several days" with the people locally in each region, that is, working in village communities. This is where John locates the base of the movement, as "many" people come to "trust" in Jesus.

References to particular villages are especially important, perhaps reflecting the fact that social memories often become solidly "attached" to particular places or persons. John specifically mentions Cana and Capernaum as important towns in Galilee, the latter mentioned also in both Mark and the Q speeches. Like the mission speech in Q, John as well mentions the overgrown village of Bethsaida, which Herod Philip had established as a "capital." In John's Gospel, Peter, Andrew, Philip, and Nathanael all come from Bethsaida (did they leave Bethsaida or go there to become leaders of the movement?). In Judea, Bethany has particular importance as the village near Jerusalem where Mary, Martha, and Lazarus were significant followers.

In all these interrelated aspects of the narrative — the wilderness feeding and other signs, Jesus' work in the countryside villages in all of the Israelite regions, the breadth of the popular (and even establishment) response to Jesus, the development of a distinctive movement that brings Jesus increasingly into conflict with the guardians of the Jerusalem great tradition — the Gospel of John portrays Jesus as engaged in the renewal of Israel. This is all the more striking in contrast to the previous understanding of the Gospel as presenting Jesus in sharp opposition to "the Jews" and "Judaism" generally. As noted above, this tragic misunderstanding is rooted in the failure to discern that "the Judeans" in John's story are those Israelites who live in Judea and often more specifically the rulers of the Judeans, the high priests and the Pharisees. Once "the Judeans," along with "the Galileans" and "the Samaritans," are understood in historical context as the people of the particular regions of Israelite heritage in Roman Palestine, however, the inclusion of all these people in the movement Jesus was generating indicates clearly that he was engaged in a renewal of Israel.

While Jesus' renewal of Israel in John's story is happening mainly among the people of the main regions of Israelite heritage and is in sharp opposition to the rulers of the Judeans, his movement of renewal was also attracting some (representative figures) of the rulers and retainers. Jesus has an extended discussion with Nicodemus, a Pharisee and "ruler of the Judeans," who "went over to Jesus" and "became one of them" (John 3:1-21; 7:50-52). The "royal officer" whose son Jesus healed became "loyal" to Jesus, along with his "whole household" (4:46-54). After Jesus' death, Joseph of Arimathea requests Jesus' body for an honorable burial (19:38). In fact, John claims that "many even of the rulers became loyal to" Jesus, although most did not confess their commitment publicly for fear that they would be excluded from the assembly of the people (12:42-43).

Finally, it is worth noting that, while John extends the scope of Jesus' renewal movement to all Israel, the Gospel appears to limit the movement to Israel. There is no clear evidence that Jesus ever speaks to or performs signs in the presence of "Gentiles." "The Greeks" who tell Philip they want to meet Jesus in Jerusalem are evidently Diaspora "Judeans/Jews" who have come on pilgrimage to the Passover festival in the temple (12:20-21; cf. 7:35). John's story thus seems to include Hellenistic Jews in the renewal of Israel, but not Gentiles.

Fulfillment of Israel's Traditions and Longings

Virtually throughout the story, the Gospel of John presents Jesus, his mission, and the response to him as deeply embedded in Israelite tradition and enacting a fulfillment of that tradition and the deep longings it expressed. He performs acts of healing and deliverance that reenact formative events in Israelite tradition and fulfill the people's hopes for new deliverance. Some of the episodes in John have parallels in the Synoptics, but are richly elaborated in John's presentation. On the basis of the new healings and the feeding, the people acclaim him as the prophet who is to come and, most prominently in John, recognize and acclaim him as "the Messiah, the king of Israel."

Usually unnoticed is that the Gospel of John presents Jesus as fulfilling Israelite tradition at two levels, as it were. In most of the narrative Jesus is fulfilling Israelite popular tradition. This can be seen most clearly perhaps in John's presentation of Jesus' actions as pointedly against or an alternative to the festivals of "the Judeans" in the Jerusalem temple or other practices of "the Judeans," that is, the official, institutionalized celebrations or practices determined and controlled by the Jerusalem rulers and their retainers. It can also be seen in the rulers' rejection of or objection to what Jesus is doing. But John presents Jesus as the fulfillment not only of Israelite popular tradition but also of official Judean tradition "written" in the Scriptures: Jesus is the one about whom Moses "wrote." We discuss in the rest of this chapter how John presents Jesus and his mission as the fulfillment of Israelite popular tradition, deferring discussion of John's presentation of his fulfillment of the official Judean scriptural tradition until the next chapter, which is devoted to Jesus' opposition to and by the Jerusalem rulers.

Enacting Renewal

In John's Gospel, somewhat as in Mark's, many of Jesus' deeds are patterned after key acts of deliverance in Israelite social memory. These episodes, individually and collectively, portray Jesus as the fulfillment of Israelite tradition, the one who satisfies the deep longings of the people for independence under the direct rule of God and a common life of justice and sufficiency. Most immediately evident, perhaps, his feeding of the multitude on the mountain in a wilderness area in anticipation of the Passover celebration of the exodus deliverance — pointedly in opposition to the official celebration in Jerusalem — is not only a richly symbolic "sign" of the renewal of Israel, but also an act of fulfillment, as the people respond: "Finally! This is what we have been longing for. This is the prophet who is to come!" (6:1-14). The ensuing discourse then elaborates on the fulfillment. Jesus thus embodies the bread of life, prefigured in the manna, the bread from heaven (vv. 32-33).

Almost as a provocation to the official regulations on Sabbath observance, John has Jesus perform two healings in Jerusalem on the Sabbath.

Certainly not coincidentally, both Sabbath healings take place at large public pools (Bethesda and Siloam) used for ceremonial washing in compliance with Judean purity regulations.[2] These acts, the healing of one man's paralysis and another's blindness, are symbolic of what Jesus is doing in the renewal of Israel generally. But they are also strongly reminiscent of the actions of the great prophets Elijah and Elisha, whose similar acts of healing would have been well known in popular Israelite tradition. Again, Jesus' (symbolic as well as concrete) acts fulfill the longings expressed in Israelite social memory. As suggested by the allusions to Israelite expectations in Jesus' response to the Baptist's disciples in Q (Luke 7:18-24), these longings included healings: "the eyes of the blind will be opened . . . the lame will leap like a deer."[3]

In addition to new acts of deliverance patterned after formative acts of deliverance, Jesus embodies-and-performs the fulfillment of hopes and expectations expressed in other Israelite tradition. A longing that had become intense in Israelite tradition during the many generations of aggressive rule by the western imperial regimes of the Seleucids and then the Romans was for restoration of the people. This was focused on images of new life and "resurrection" of the people (in general), of which the "resurrection" of ancestors and the vindication of martyrs were components (see, e.g., Dan 12:1-3). Jesus' raising of Lazarus is clearly a fulfillment of just this longing for restoration to new life, and his self-identification as "the resurrection and the life" is an assertion that in his mission the longed-for restoration of the people to life has come (11:17-44).

While it may be less obvious, Jesus' first sign in Galilee, the transfor-

---

2. See Urban von Wahlde, "Archaeology and John's Gospel," pages 523-86 in *Jesus and Archaeology*, ed. James Charlesworth (Grand Rapids: Eerdmans, 2006), 564-66; "The Puzzling Pool of Bethesda," *Biblical Archaeology Review* 37.5 (September/October 2011), 40-46, 65.

3. Traditionally, the articulations of the people's longings for renewal at Luke 7:22-24 have been understood as "quotations" of Scripture, perhaps Isa 35:5-6 or 61:1-2, despite the fact that Jesus' words do not match any particular text from the Old Testament. It seems more likely that Jesus is summarizing the general longings of the people under the effects of imperial conquest and domination and that Isa 35:5-6 and 61:1-2 represent prophetic/scribal reflections on the same popular theme. See here Richard Horsley, "Q and Israelite Tradition," in *Performance in Text and Tradition* (Eugene: Cascade, 2013), chapter 6.

mation of water to wine at the wedding feast in Cana, is yet another act in fulfillment of hopes and longings rooted in Israelite tradition. Again John sets up his act in pointed juxtaposition to the Judean rites of purification for which water was stored in the jars (2:6). Among the many highly symbolic terms and concepts in John's account of this first sign, marriage was a long-standing symbol of the union between the people and their God. As is clear from the analogy used in the episode about (not) fasting in Mark 2:18-20, the future wedding feast had become a prime symbol of the hoped-for future celebration of the union of God's anointed (or prophet) and the renewed people of Israel, as the bridegroom and the bride. The first episode in Jesus' mission in John indicates that the fulfillment of this longing has come. In these signs and other acts of Jesus, John presents not only a renewal of the people but a fulfillment of their longings expressed in Israelite tradition for new life of divine restoration and provision.

The Prophet/Messiah of Renewal

Prominent among the symbols and expressions of the renewal of Israel that Jesus is effecting are the roles and "titles" in which he is acclaimed. In the introduction to the story (John 1) both the Baptist and prominent followers of Jesus refer to him in deeply symbolic terms that anticipate his engagement in a renewal of Israel and his fulfillment of Israel's hopes. While a number of these terms — "Lamb of God" (v. 36), "Messiah/Christ" (v. 41), "Son of God" (v. 49), "Son of Man" (used by Jesus of himself, v. 51) — have taken on a life of their own in the history of Christian theology, it is important to understand them in the historical and narrative contexts in which John uses them.

In the past half-century biblical scholarship has shown that ancient Judean texts exhibit great diversity in speaking of future (or current) "anointed ones" and/or "prophets."[4] Indeed, references to some sort of

4. Among the many studies contributing to the dismantling of the synthetic theological construct of "Jewish expectations" of "the Messiah," see the papers from the 1987 Princeton Symposium *The Messiah: Developments in Earliest Judaism and Christianity,* ed. James H. Charlesworth (Minneapolis: Fortress, 1992); and Jacob Neusner et al., eds.,

anticipated "anointed" figure are rare in late second temple Judean texts, and references to a coming "prophet" of some sort are also relatively rare. Further, when the terms "anointed" or "prophet" are used, they typically refer to an anticipated *function* or political-religious *role* and less to the specific figure(s) who will enact it. While there is little evidence in scribal texts that the elite expected a/the "messiah" or "prophet," and even less that "the Messiah" was an established title for an anticipated figure, it is all the more striking that the people produced several movements led by popular prophets and "kings," as outlined in chapter 1. Overall, the evidence suggests that terms such as "messiah" and "prophet" should be understood in primarily social/relational terms, as words that refer to roles and functions of renewal figures rather than as fixed Christological "titles" that John adopted to attribute abstract theological values to Jesus. As will be seen in the review below, John's story tends to use "messiah," "prophet," and similar labels less as ontological "titles" and more as categories in which Jesus speaks and acts in effecting the renewal of the people.

At the outset of the story, the Baptist says that he came baptizing so that Jesus might be "revealed to Israel" (1:31). Seeing Jesus, John acclaims him "the lamb of God" and "the chosen one" (v. 34).[5] Andrew, one of John's disciples, then eagerly tells his brother Simon Peter, "we have found 'the Messiah' (which is translated as 'the anointed one')" (v. 41). After Jesus goes to Galilee, Nathanael, explicitly identified as "an Israelite," acclaims the rabbi/teacher Jesus as "the Son of God, the king of Israel!" (v. 49). The presentation gives the sense that these monikers all refer to the same role, the "king of Israel" who is also "the anointed" "son of God" (vv. 29, 34, 41, 47-49), a role that would have been well known among

---

Judaisms and Their Messiahs (Cambridge: Cambridge University Press, 1988). For an attempt to restore the older synthetic concept with variations based on Judean scribal texts, see John J. Collins, *The Scepter and the Star: Messianism in Light of the Dead Sea Scrolls* (2nd ed.; Grand Rapids: Eerdmans, 1995).

5. While the manuscript evidence is fairly evenly weighted, the reading "chosen one" is to be preferred over "Son of God" at John 1:34 (contra the 27th ed. of the Nestle-Aland text). While both terms are consistent with Johannine theology, the former would more likely reflect the worldview of John the Baptist, and it is difficult to explain why Christian scribes would change "Son of God" to the less impressive "chosen one."

those familiar with Israelite tradition (see 2 Samuel 7; Psalms 2 and 110). Jesus himself then tells Nathanael that he will see "heaven opened and divine messengers ascending and descending upon the son of man" (1:51). From John the Baptist's insistence that he himself not only is not "the Messiah" but also not "the prophet," it seems clear that "the/a prophet" is also an important role from Israelite tradition that a future figure will fulfill (1:20-21). That "the Judeans"/Pharisees have sent priests and Levites to interrogate the Baptist regarding his own role suggests also that these roles were a threat to the established order that the Jerusalem rulers were charged to maintain (vv. 19, 25).

That Jesus does indeed fulfill the role of "the anointed one," "the king of Israel," becomes increasingly evident in the course of the story. The Gospel concludes with the declaration that the story was written just so that its audiences would trust that Jesus is indeed "the Messiah, the Son of God" (12:12-15; 20:30-31). Accordingly, John's narrative affirms at many prominent points this fulfillment of hopes and expectations and Jesus' main role as the Messiah engaged in a renewal of Israel. To the Samaritan woman's declaration that she knows "Messiah is coming," Jesus responds, "I, the one speaking to you, am he" (4:25-26, cf. v. 29). That the people are eager for the kind of leadership that Jesus offers, a leadership that fits the tradition of popularly anointed ones, is indicated in John's note that the crowds "were about . . . to make him king" after the feeding miracle (6:15). The Judeans who witness what Jesus does and says suspect that their rulers really know (but are concealing) that Jesus is "the Messiah." "When the Messiah comes, will he do more signs than this man has done?" (7:26-27, 31); apparently granting the point, Jesus' detractors can only insist that surely "the Messiah does not come from Galilee (as does Jesus)," for the Scripture says that he is to be a descendant of David and hence should come from David's village Bethlehem (in Judea, vv. 41-42). At the festival of Dedication, the Judeans, who clearly recognize what Jesus is doing, demand that he identify himself: "If you are the Messiah, tell us plainly" (10:24). He does not, but Martha subsequently states unambiguously that "you are the Messiah, the Son of God, the one coming into the world" (11:27). Jesus' role as the one who has been anointed by God to effect renewal emerges most prominently in the "triumphal entry" into Jerusalem, when he is acclaimed "king of Israel" by a great crowd of Passover pilgrims (12:13), much to the dismay of the priests and Pharisees (v. 19).

To implement his main role as "anointed one," bringing life and salvation to the world in the renewal of Israel, Jesus is also "the Son of Man." While John never uses this term to describe Jesus and very rarely (compared to the Synoptics) shows Jesus using it of himself, "Son of Man" notably appears at points in the story where Jesus' mission of renewal and restoration is center stage. Thus, Jesus tells his new disciples, who have just acclaimed him "Messiah," "Son of God," and "king of Israel" (1:41, 49), that they "will see the heavens opened and angels of God going up and down on the Son of Man," a promise that is immediately fulfilled not in a mystical visionary ascent but rather in the transformation of water to wine (2:1-11).

In the discourse following the healing of the lame man at Bethesda, Jesus borrows a common motif from Israel's prophetic tradition to compare his life-giving ministry to the anticipated resurrection/restoration of the people: "An hour comes, and now is here, when the dead will hear the voice of the Son of God and live. . . . The Father has given him authority to judge, because he is Son of Man" (5:26-27) — words that clearly refer, in this context, not to some distant eschatological event but rather to the renewal that is taking place already in Jesus' work.

The same theme reemerges in the second Sabbath healing (9:35-39), as the once-blind man, having been put out of the assembly by the Pharisees for refusing to condemn Jesus, prostrates himself in reverence before "the Son of Man" who has restored his sight and who promises that he, unlike the false shepherds of Israel (the Judean rulers, 10:7-18), "will never cast out" those who come to him (6:37).

Jesus notably refers to himself as "Son of Man" three times in the "bread from heaven" discourse following the miraculous feeding (6:27, 53, 62), where Jesus, earlier acclaimed by the people as a prophet (v. 14), urges the people to "work for the bread that remains into eternal life" (v. 27). Particularly poignant and distinctive in the Gospel of John is that Jesus is seen as "the Son of Man" in his crucifixion, the time when he will be "lifted up" to "draw all people to myself" — that is, to restore all the people of Israel in one united flock (3:13-14; 6:27, 62; 8:28; 12:23, 31-34).

While his main role is that of "the Messiah, king of Israel," Jesus also at several points acts in the role of a/the prophet, as recognized by characters who witness his actions. The Samaritan woman at Jacob's well recognizes him as a prophet because of his knowledge of her previous life (4:29). Jesus himself knows he is a prophet (v. 44), and his feeding of the multitude on the mountain is clearly the act of a prophet — the new Moses — as evident both from the people's acclamation "this is indeed the prophet who is to come into the world" (6:14) and Jesus' own lengthy commentary on the sign, in which he compares what he has done to the provision of manna in the wilderness (vv. 24-58). The impressive speech and actions of Jesus leave some people unclear about his role, whether "this is the prophet" or "the Messiah" (7:40-41). He impresses the Judeans as a bit of both, and the feeble protests of the Pharisees, who clearly know of a prophet in Israelite expectation but insist that none is to arise in Galilee, function in the narrative as a confirmation that he is indeed a prophet (v. 52). Although not all prophets would heal — John the Baptist, for instance, "did no sign" (10:41) — and while not all healers would necessarily be prophets, Israelite tradition did associate healing with some prophets, particularly the great archetypal renewal prophets Elijah and Elisha. The blind man whose eyes Jesus has opened sees the connection, recognizing that one with such healing powers "is a prophet" (9:17), but other characters in the story indicate that "the prophet (who is to come into the world)" would have other functions as well, such as feeding and teaching the people (6:14; 7:40).

Mark and Q both represent Jesus (mainly or exclusively) as a prophet, as discussed in chapter 3 above. Mark's story portrays him as a prophet like both Moses and Elijah, as manifested in his act of power in renewal of the people; Q presents Jesus as the new Moses enacting a renewal of the Mosaic covenant and a prophet who delivers oracles and woes in traditional prophetic forms. Jesus' identity as a prophet is also prominent and explicit in John's story, even where he is presented primarily as "the messiah," a fact that serves to further confirm Mark's and Q's portrayal of him as a prophet from early tradition about Jesus. That Jesus, in interacting with his followers and in opposition to the rulers, worked in the traditional role of a prophet leading a movement of renewal also fits the historical context. As noted in chapter 1, several popular prophets led movements of renewal in the Judean and Samaritan countryside clearly informed by or patterned after the formative acts of deliverance led by the prototypical prophet Moses (and/or Joshua).

It is important to stress once more, with regard to Jesus' fulfillment of key titles and roles, that all is presented relationally in the story. While the Johannine Jesus has often been portrayed as aloof and distant, the "man from heaven" who makes abstract theological declarations about the various ways that he embodies life and salvation ("I am the way, the truth, and the life," etc.), the characters in John's story identify Jesus as "messiah" and/or "prophet" in response to his actions and words that impact their lives. They speak as representatives of the larger group of those who come to place their trust *(pisteuein)* in Jesus, not in the sense of being "converted" to him but in the sense of giving their loyalty to him and to the renewal that he is accomplishing.

John's presentation of Jesus as "Messiah, king of Israel" is distinctive among the Gospels, unparalleled in Mark and Q. The sequence of speeches in Q knows nothing of Jesus as "anointed" or a "king." In Mark, when Peter acclaims him as "the Messiah," Jesus rebukes him: "get behind me, Satan" (Mark 8:27-33). Further along in Mark's story, Jesus pointedly rejects James and John's anticipation that he will become king and award them positions of power (10:35-45). And Mark has Jesus publicly challenge the idea that the Messiah will necessarily be "the son of David," at least according to conventional conceptions (12:35-37). One can readily understand why Wilhelm Wrede and subsequent interpreters would assert that "the messianic secret" is key to the Gospel of Mark, for if Jesus were the Messiah, Mark certainly keeps it secret![6] Matthew and Luke do give more play to Jesus as the Messiah as well as a prophet, but do not portray "messiah" as his primary role-and-title and do not make the development of this theme primary to the overall story in the distinctive way that John does.

Finally, it is important to note that the presentation of Jesus as the Messiah in John's story cannot be explained simply as a later "christological" development. The Gospel has expanded the role-and-title to include far more than is indicated in any of the relatively rare references to

6. The classic and highly influential study originally published in 1901 was Wilhelm Wrede, *The Messianic Secret,* trans. J. C. G. Greig (Greenwood: Attic, 1971).

an anointed figure in Judean texts of the time. Understanding Jesus as a/ the messiah, however, was an early tradition. It was certainly earlier than the apostle Paul, insofar as he knows "Christ" as not so much a title as part of a name, "Jesus Christ," whose title is "Lord." Mark, moreover, clearly knows that Jesus was understood by some as "messiah" or "king," as evident in his pointed rejection or serious qualification of this understanding. Furthermore, the several popular kings who led revolts against Roman rule in 4 BCE after the death of Herod, as mentioned by Josephus, indicate that the role was very much alive among Israelites in Galilee and the Transjordan as well as in Judea. John includes a brief reference that might be a reminiscence that some people had responded to Jesus in similar terms, wanting "to take him by force and make him king" (6:15). Like the popular kings, John's Jesus heads a movement of renewal and resistance to the rulers. Although he was not leading a revolt, John's "king of Israel" was killed by a Roman form of execution specifically for rebel leaders. And in their council about what to do about Jesus' movement, the high priests and Pharisees are worried that the Romans will "come and destroy . . . our people" as they had in suppressing the earlier revolts led by popularly acclaimed "kings." The Gospel of John presents a bold portrayal of Jesus as "the Messiah" leading the people in renewal and resistance, which is a distinctive view among the Gospels.

CHAPTER EIGHT

The Prophet/Messiah and the Rulers of Israel

O ur investigation has led to the important conclusion that the Gospel of John presents Jesus as sharply opposed to and by "the Judeans," who are synonymous with the high priests and Pharisees, the "rulers" of the Jerusalem temple-state under the oversight of the Roman governor. The reading of John as presenting Jesus versus "the Jews" generally is a carryover from an older theological scheme of Christian origins in which Jesus was understood as the great revealer whose teaching and crucifixion led to the emergence of one religion, Christianity, from another, Judaism. The basis of that reading, perpetuated in recent translations such as the New Revised Standard Version and the Jerusalem Bible, is the (mis-)translation of the term *hoi Ioudaioi* as "the Jews." Investigation of word usage (see chapter 2), however, shows that while outsiders such as the Romans may have referred to people of Israelite heritage generally as "the Judeans," insiders referred to them more precisely according to the different regions in which people of Israelite heritage lived as "the Judeans," "the Samaritans," and "the Galileans."

If we read the Gospel of John in the context of insider culture of the first century CE, it is clear that, like Josephus's histories, it makes these geographical distinctions. But it also often uses "the Judeans" in a narrower sense in reference to the rulers of the Judeans, specifically "the high priests and the Pharisees." It is thus necessary to attend carefully and critically to the narrative context to determine whom the story is referring to. At points, when Jesus is working in the countryside or interacting with festival crowds, "many" of "the Judeans" become loyal to him. But more often "the Judeans" are the rulers of the Jerusalem temple-state whom Jesus opposes and who are seeking to kill him. Thus it should be clear that in the Gospel of John, Jesus is not attacking "Judaism" and "the Jews" generally. In fact he is doing virtually the opposite: Jesus is generating a renewal of Israel in fulfillment of the deep longings expressed in Israelite culture, a renewal that includes Judeans as well as Galileans and even Samaritans.

The Gospel of John does, however, portray Jesus' actions and teaching in renewal of Israel as directly opposed to and opposed by "the Judeans" as a narrower reference to the high priests and Pharisees in charge of the Jerusalem temple under the oversight of the Roman governor. The sharpness of Jesus' attacks and of the reaction by the Judean rulers cannot be downplayed. But it may be more comprehensible if understood in the historical context of late second temple Judea-Samaria-Galilee in which the temple and the high priests became increasingly unpopular in Jerusalem scribal circles as well as among the people as the high priests collaborated with their imperial patrons and became ever more exploitative of the people.

People and Scribes against the High Priestly Rulers

Chapter 1 surveyed the fundamental division between rulers and ruled in early Roman Palestine, including the widespread popular revolts of 4 BCE and 66-72 CE and the many smaller-scale protests and movements of resistance among both the villagers and scribal circles. But it may help clarify the historical context further to supplement that presentation with a review of the negative attitude toward the high priests and even the temple articulated in many second temple Judean texts. In particular it may serve to clarify some of the misunderstanding resulting from one recent line of interpretation of Jesus' prophetic condemnation of the temple. Contending that Jesus was promising to build a new temple after destroying the old one, E. P. Sanders claims that there was a long tradition of expectation of a rebuilt temple in prophetic and apocalyptic texts.[1] Such a claim, however, is not attested in the key texts Sanders cites, while most Judean texts indicate both popular and scribal opposition to the high priestly rulers in Jerusalem.

Opposition to Jerusalem rulers runs deep in Israelite tradition. The Deuteronomic history produced by scribes serving in the latter years of the Davidic monarchy or in the temple-state includes stories of widespread revolts against David himself, once he consolidated power in Jerusalem, and the revolt of the northern Israelites against Solomon's forced labor for construction of the temple and royal palaces (2 Samuel 15–18, 20; 1 Kings 11–12). Elijah and Elisha led prophetic and popular resistance to the oppressive king Ahab in Samaria (1 Kings 17–21; 2 Kings 1–9). Amos and Hosea in the north and Micah and Isaiah in the south pronounced God's condemnation on kings and their officers, including their lavish temple rituals, for oppressing the people (e.g., Isaiah 3:13-15; 5). Jeremiah pronounced God's condemnation on the Davidic kings for economic exploitation of the people and of the temple in violation of the commandments of the Mosaic covenant (Jeremiah 7; 22; 26). After these prophecies were fulfilled in the Babylonian destruction of Jerusalem and its temple and the termination of the Davidic dynasty, the temple-state was reestablished in Jerusalem under Persian sponsorship as an instrument of imperial control and taxation as well as worship of "the God who is in Jerusalem" (Ezra 1). The establishment prophet Haggai supported the rebuilding of the temple with a glowing imperial ideology, but the very fact that he would need to encourage the people to surrender their labor and produce indicates clearly that many were not enthused about the project (Haggai 1–2). A century later, the governor Nehemiah, sent by the Persians with military enforcers, had to forcibly check the Judean elite to mitigate their exploitation of the people (Neh 5:1-13).

---

1. E. P. Sanders, *Jesus and Judaism* (Philadelphia: Fortress, 1985), chapter 2. See the review and refutation in Richard Horsley, *Jesus and the Spiral of Violence: Popular Jewish Resistance in Roman Palestine* (San Francisco: Harper & Row, 1987), 289-91. See now the broader context and further critical analysis of key texts in Richard Horsley, *Scribes, Visionaries, and the Politics of Second Temple Judea* (Louisville: Westminster John Knox, 2007), especially chapters 8 and 9; *Revolt of the Scribes: Resistance and Apocalyptic Origins* (Minneapolis: Fortress, 2010).

When our Judean sources for Judean history resume in the late third and second centuries BCE under the Hellenistic empires, it is evident that not just ordinary people (e.g., those involved in the Maccabean revolt) but also several dissident scribal circles had turned against their aristocratic patrons, the high priests, with some coming close to rejecting the second temple itself as illegitimate. The historical visions and interpretations of Daniel 7, 8, and 10–12 envision a future restoration of the people that does not include a temple, and no temple is mentioned in the vision of restoration in *Testament of Moses* 10. Similarly, in the "Enoch" texts, especially the Animal Vision (*1 Enoch* 85–90), the future restoration includes a large "house" (the people) but no "tower" (the temple), and the second temple is declared to be corrupt, with "polluted bread" on the altar (*1 Enoch* 89:73; 90:28-29).[2]

If the reforming high priests were viewed as instruments of imperial rule, the Hasmoneans who rode the Maccabean revolt to power were usurpers. While willing to serve in the regime of cooperative Hasmoneans, however, the Pharisees evidently turned against the expansionist wars of Alexander Yannai, leading to a virtual civil war in the early first century BCE (*Antiquities* 13.372-97). After Herod made the temple and the high priests into instruments of his own rule, the people clamored for the appointment of a more just high priest, which was about all they could do under threat of violence — until the widespread revolts broke out in 4 BCE.

Closer to the time of Jesus, the *Psalms of Solomon* envision no place for the temple in the future restoration of the people. The trampling of the altar by alien nations (Pompey) is viewed as just punishment for the Hasmonean high priests (2:2-3; 8:10-13, 20-25). After the Messiah liberates Jerusalem/Israel/the people from foreign domination and purges them of injustice, "the place" where the Lord will be glorified is not the temple but rather "Zion/Jerusalem/the holy mountain" (*Psalms of Solomon* 17), and the dwelling of God is to be in the midst of the people, the

2. The claim that the Ten-Week Vision in *1 Enoch* 93:1-10; 91:11-17 anticipates a rebuilt temple is based on a problematic reconstruction of the text of 91:13. As in *1 Enoch* 90:28-29, the "house" is a symbol for the restored people, not for the temple (the "tower"). See here George W. E. Nickelsberg, *1 Enoch* vol. 1 (Hermeneia; Minneapolis: Fortress, 2001), 434-37.

house of Jacob, who are God's "holy inheritance" (7:1-2, 5, 9). The scribal-priestly community formed in the wilderness at Qumran rejected the incumbent high priesthood and understood the community itself as the (real, replacement) temple and their righteous community life as its "sacrifices."

Indeed, other than Sirach, it is difficult to find any Judean texts that offer vocal support of the high priests and temple, although the Pharisees and other scribes, probably the majority of them, still served the temple-state. The more critical scribes and Pharisees, on the other hand, mounted active resistance, as in the "Fourth Philosophy" and the Sicarii, who even assassinated key high priestly figures who were collaborating too closely with the Romans.

If even some scribes, whose role was to serve the temple-state, opposed the incumbent high priests and questioned or rejected the temple, it would be difficult to imagine that Israelite villagers constrained to render tithes and offerings in support of the temple and its presiding priests were universally supportive of the ruling institutions. Still underway was the rebuilding of the temple in grand Hellenistic-Roman style, which must have been alienating to the people. The families of the men that Herod had elevated to the high priesthood formed the enlarged priestly aristocracy from which the Roman governors appointed successive high priests. The first-century high priestly rulers thus lacked legitimacy in the eyes of the people from the outset. Josephus's accounts of affairs in the first century, particularly the behavior of the high priestly aristocracy under the Roman governors, is a story of steady deterioration of public order under increasingly dysfunctional and sometimes predatory rulers.[3] Such is the historical context in which the Gospel of John's portrayal of the opposition between Jesus and the rulers of the Judeans should be understood.

---

3. Martin Goodman, *The Ruling Class of Judaea: The Origins of the Jewish Revolt against Rome A.D. 66-70* (Cambridge: Cambridge University Press, 1987), lays out in some detail how the high priestly "ruling class" became increasingly illegitimate in the first century CE.

Jesus' Demonstration against the Temple Emporium

Christian readers of the Fourth Gospel, whose sense of Christ's career has been shaped mainly by the Synoptics, have long been puzzled by John's placement of Jesus' demonstration against the temple near the very beginning of the story (John 2:13-20). The pre-Jerusalem narratives and speeches in the Synoptics take place in Galilee and nearby areas far to the north. Not surprisingly, then, the Synoptic Jesus is only rarely in direct conflict with the Judean rulers, aside from statements that the Pharisees are out to get him and his own brief prophetic condemnation of the ruling house of Jerusalem and of the role of the Pharisees. Only after delivering most of his teaching and performing all of his healings and exorcisms does Jesus go up to Jerusalem in a "triumphal entry," where he carries out a "cleansing of the temple" followed by the climactic events of "the Passion narrative."

In neither John nor the Synoptics, of course, was Jesus' dramatic action a "cleansing of the temple." The Temple was indeed a massive institution in which extensive sacrifices and offerings were presented to God by the presiding priests. But those sacrifices and offerings point to the temple's central role in the economy of Judea, a role that was only enhanced by the fact that the Jerusalem priests were also the political "heads of state" set in place by the Romans. Further, the temple served as a sacred bank in which sacrifices, offerings, and other gifts accumulated and in which the elite deposited most of their wealth. Both John and Mark portray Jesus' action in the temple as an obstruction of the religious-economic business connected with the sacrifices, such as the sale of sheep and cattle and money changing.[4] His forcible, disruptive action in the temple is shocking enough. That he carries out this action at the very beginning of his mission in John's story is simply astounding. Just after the seemingly innocuous changing of water to wine, John's Jesus mounts a forcible public obstruction of business in the temple that should have resulted in his immediate seizure and execution.

John's account of Jesus' action makes it sound even more ominous

---

4. See the discussion of such business as entailed in the sacrifices performed in the temple in Sanders, *Jesus and Judaism,* especially pp. 61-65.

and forcible than does Mark's account. The latter has Jesus not allowing anyone through the temple courtyard, while John's Jesus makes a whip of cords with which to drive them out, in addition to overturning the tables of the money changers. His charge in John's account is a sharp condemnation of the exploitation of the people for the benefit of the ruling elite: "Stop making my Father's house a house of emporium" (2:16). An "emporium" in the Roman Empire and the ancient Near East was trade carried out for the benefit of the wealthy and powerful, with luxury goods brought by traders in caravans and ships from afar, where they had been produced by other peoples subordinated to the imperial order. The massive reconstruction of the temple and the whole temple mount by Herod had transformed the complex into a sacred political-economic institution and global pilgrimage site, one of the wonders of the Roman imperial world. In a provincial capital such as Jerusalem, the word "emporium" carried connotations of something foreign that did not belong there, certainly not in the eyes of villagers who knew very well how their rulers came by the resources to "trade" for the luxurious goods they desired.

Interpreters have often taken the parenthetical "aside" that "he was speaking about the temple of his body" (2:21), clearly an allusion to his upcoming death and resurrection, as a way of "explaining away" Jesus' blatant political-economic-religious disruption and his declaration about the destruction and raising up of the temple. This is hardly the case, however, considering the way discourse proceeds at a double level in John's story, as the highly symbolic Jesus and the literal-minded Judeans and Nicodemus (et al.) talk past one another, and the way in which the meaning of earlier episodes gradually unfolds with illumination from subsequent episodes and dialogues. Also at play in this episode is the double (or multiple!) meaning of "house" in Israelite tradition and in the context of a prophet (or messiah) engaged in the renewal of Israel. The "house" that they are making into a house of emporium can be the temple, the "house of God." But in Israelite tradition and particularly in the key texts surveyed earlier, "house" is a symbol of the people, and *not* of the temple.

In this case, John's Jesus may be juxtaposing and playing on "house" in both of these senses. In the buying and selling and money changing in the temple the Judean rulers are turning the people of Israel into an emporium for the benefit of the elite at the expense of the people. In saying "[if you] Destroy this sanctuary . . ." Jesus means that they, the Judean rulers, are destroying God's sanctuary, that is, the people of Israel. The meaning of "in three days I will raise it up" is at this point in the story not yet clear. But the aside that in the sanctuary raised up he was referring to the sanctuary of his body looks forward to the highly symbolic discourse yet to come in the Gospel story, particularly to the way Jesus would die raised up on a cross. And that, as any reader/hearer of the story already knows, is just what would happen to a prophet/messiah who took such bold brazen public action in blockading the temple. And that, as John's Jesus explains toward the end of the ensuing dialogue with Nicodemus, is how the Son could become salvation for those who would become loyal to him (3:16-17).

The presentation of Jesus' attack on the temple toward the beginning of his mission not only heightens the impact of this prophetic act, but gives the clear signal that Jesus was generating the renewal of Israel in adamant opposition to the Judean ruling institution of temple and high priesthood. Just this "sign" along with the others led many among those in Jerusalem and among those back in Galilee to become loyal to Jesus (2:23; 4:45). Having indicated in no uncertain terms that Jesus' renewal of Israel is in direct opposition to the Judean rulers, John's story proceeds to all of the related ways in which Jesus is challenging and rejecting the rulers, ruling institutions, and their use of the official law and Scripture to control the people.

Replacing the Temple

While the episodes that immediately follow the temple incident do not involve direct confrontations with the Judean rulers, they do show Jesus overtly challenging the ruling institution of the temple and the festivals of the Judeans controlled by the high priests and Pharisees. Like that of his predecessor John the Baptist (see 1:19-24), Jesus' baptizing activity in the countryside villages of Judea presents the people with an alternate form of purification, one that is connected to his own movement and thus that arouses the suspicion of the Pharisees, who apparently succeed in pressuring Jesus to leave the region (3:22; 4:1-3). In both his conversation with the Samaritan woman at Jacob's well and in his feeding of the multitude at Passover on the mountain on the other side of the Sea of Galilee, Jesus declares or enacts an alternative to worship and festivals in the temple in the renewal of Israel that he is generating (4:21-24). Neither of these episodes is explainable as a post-resurrection invention of the church, much less as a "Christian" rejection of the "Jewish" temple following the Roman destruction of Jerusalem. Both accounts are deeply rooted in Israelite tradition, and both make sense in the context of the historical relations between the Jerusalem temple/high priesthood and the Samaritans and Galileans, respectively, in Jesus' time. In the larger flow of John's narrative, both the Samaritan mission and the feeding are integral steps in Jesus' renewal of Israel against the rulers of Israel.

The setting of Jesus' conversation with the Samaritan woman, "Jacob's well" outside the village of "Sychar, near the plot of ancestral land that Jacob had given to his son Joseph" (4:5), is a pointed inclusion of the Samaritan version of popular Israelite tradition in Jesus' renewal of all Israel. It is in direct opposition to the suppression or exclusion of that part of common Israelite tradition by the Jerusalem-based official "Judean" tradition. Jacob/Israel was, as the woman notes (v. 20), the common ancestor of all Israel; Joseph was one of the twelve eponymous ancestors of Israelites in the central hill country. A people's tradition, their common social memory, is often attached to particular places or "landmarks" that (metonymically) evoke a whole complex of values, values that are often essential to the group's identity.[5] The ancestral land that Jacob/Israel had given Joseph had long been a central landmark of Samaritan identity as Israelite people. In connection with the Judean high priesthood's conquest of the Samaritans and destruction of their temple on Mount Gerizim, however, the scribal and priestly custodians of the official Judean tradition that served to legitimate the Jerusalem temple as *the* (only) place where God could be properly served (with tithes and offerings as well as loyalty) had downplayed or perhaps even attempted to

5. See especially Maurice Halbwachs, *On Collective Memory,* ed. and trans. Lewis Coser (Chicago: University of Chicago Press, 1992), 193-235; Yael Zerubavel, *Recovered Roots: Collective Memory and the Making of Israeli National Tradition* (Chicago: University of Chicago Press, 1995), offers a particularly helpful discussion of the role of landmark events and places in group consciousness.

suppress this high-value Samaritan "landmark" in Israelite tradition. This episode in John's story of Jesus' step by step generation of the renewal of Israel, however, pointedly reincorporates this central Samaritan landmark into the general popular Israelite tradition that all renewed Israel would thus share.

Further, and more explicitly, Jesus' conversation with the Samaritan woman is the occasion for his declaration that the temple, claimed by the Judean rulers as the only place where God can be properly worshiped, is only a temporary, historical institution. "The hour is coming, *and is now here*," when God will be worshiped neither on the sacred mountain of Samaria nor in Jerusalem, but "in spirit and truth" — that is, without any centralizing sacred institution (4:21-24). In this declaration about the state of worship in the renewal of Israel, Jesus would only have been articulating the attitudes of many other Israelites at the time. The Samaritans had a deeply rooted historical basis for rejecting the temple in Jerusalem and the Judean rulers' claims for it, and, as noted earlier, it is questionable whether the Galileans would have developed much of an attachment to the Jerusalem priesthood during the century in which they had been ruled by the expansionist Hasmoneans and then Herod, after whose death the Galileans in the area around Nazareth had revolted. As noted earlier, even some circles of scribes whose profession was to serve as advisers in the temple-state had envisioned a restoration of the people following the end of imperial rule that pointedly did not include the centralizing institution of the temple. With worship of God decentralized and reconstituted in a renewal of all Jacob's children, the boundaries between Judeans and Samaritans could be collapsed.

In John's story, Jesus again rejects the temple and what it represents by pointedly staging the feeding in the wilderness at the time of "the Passover festival of the Judeans" celebrated in Jerusalem (6:1-14).[6] The Passover, a symbolic celebration of the people's liberation from subjection to alien rulers in the exodus, was originally a festival observed in families/households in village communities, as noted above. The requirement that

6. For a helpful overview of the correlation between episodes in John's Gospel and the festivals in the temple, see Gale Yee, *Jewish Feasts and the Gospel of John* (Wilmington: Michael Glazier, 1989).

the people come up to Jerusalem and the temple for the festival was a centralization of religious-economic power. It is unclear to what degree Galileans were expected to make the (three-week) journey to Jerusalem, and whether or how often many of them did. In staging a Passover feeding in the wilderness, juxtaposing memory of another major "event" of the exodus with the commemoration of the sea-crossing itself as part of his renewal of Israel, Jesus enacted an alternative to the celebration of Passover in the Jerusalem temple. His renewal of Israel was a declaration of independence from the ruling institutions of Jerusalem.

The celebration of an alternative Passover as a wilderness feeding on the mountain in rejection of the temple leads to Jesus' declaration that he embodies "the bread of God that gives life to the world" (6:32-40), just as the reincorporation of Joseph's ancestral land and Jacob's well that had been suppressed in the official tradition led to the replacement of worship in the Jerusalem temple with worship in spirit and truth. Both episodes clarify what was happening in Jesus' attack on the temple and his statement "Destroy this sanctuary and I will raise it up." It should now be clearer that the "explanation" that Jesus was referring to his "body" that would surely be crucified for having attacked the temple was by no means a lessening of just how politically-economically and religiously ominous his attack on the temple was. That attack, his embodiment of the bread of life, and his crucifixion (his raising/exaltation on the cross) have everything to do with the renewal of Israel in opposition to the ruling institutions.

Jesus, the Law, and the "Disciples of Moses"

Both of Jesus' healings in Jerusalem in John's story are staged to provoke the Judean rulers, particularly the Pharisees. In contrast to the healing episodes in Mark, John's Jesus expresses no particular compassion for the lame man and the blind man, who have been suffering virtually all their lives, nor do either of these individuals express any level of faith in Jesus before he heals them. After being healed, one man does not come to trust in Jesus, while the other is expelled from the assembly because of his commitment to Jesus.

That the healing of the crippled man (5:1-9) is a provocation is clearly signaled by its setting at (another) "festival of the Judeans" — the pool with five porticoes at Bethzatha/Bethesda, a large public facility immediately north of the temple complex where people purified themselves before entering the temple during festivals. Jesus goes to this place where many sick people can be found (5:3) on a Sabbath (v. 9), clearly intending to challenge the official Sabbath regulations by healing someone. To add to the provocation, moreover, he commands the man to "stand up, take your mat, and walk!" — another violation of the Sabbath laws. The (anticipated) objections of the Judean officials provide a foil for Jesus' sharp criticism of "the Scriptures"/ the law to which they look to as their authority and legitimation.

The escalating conflict that continues through the next few episodes leads to Jesus' further provocation in the second healing, of a blind man, again pointedly on a Sabbath (9:1-7; cf. 7:2, 10-11). As Jesus leaves the temple complex to avoid being stoned, the disciples articulate the new challenge that Jesus' healing of the blind man is about to pose to the Judeans/Pharisees: "Who sinned, this man or his parents, so that he should be born blind?" (9:1-2). Jesus' answer, "Neither this man nor his parents sinned," bluntly contradicts the official teaching that sickness is a result of sin. To add to the provocation, moreover, Jesus engages in work on the Sabbath by making mud out of spit and dirt and spreading it on the man's eyes. He then tells the man to travel to the pool of Siloam, another large purification pool south of the temple complex, to wash himself.[7] As might be expected from this multiple provocation in violation of the official law and its understanding, the Pharisees conclude that Jesus is a "sinner" (i.e., a Sabbath-breaker, 9:16, 24).

In both healings — on Sabbath, at festival time, in Jerusalem, at pools for purification, near the temple — Jesus is clearly challenging the

---

7. See, e.g., Ronny Reich and Eli Shukron, "The Siloam Pool in the Wake of Recent Discoveries," *New Studies on Jerusalem* 10 (2004), 137-39; Urban von Wahlde, "The Pool of Siloam: The Importance of the New Discoveries for Our Understanding of Ritual Immersion in Late Second Temple Judaism and the Gospel of John," pages 155-74 in *John, Jesus, and History 2: Aspects of Historicity in the Fourth Gospel,* ed. Paul Anderson, Felix Just, and Tom Thatcher (Early Christianity and Its Literature 2; Atlanta: Society of Biblical Literature, 2009).

whole complex of temple festivals, Sabbath regulations, and the law that the rulers of the Judeans view as authoritative, as the Scripture that legitimates their position and gives them authority as its enforcers. Now the rulers of the Judeans who did not arrest Jesus after his attack on the temple attempt to seize and/or stone him and threaten to expel from the assembly of the people anyone who becomes loyal to him (5:18; 7:32; 8:59; 9:22; cf. 10:39).

After he heals the crippled man, the Judean rulers charge both Jesus and the man with breaking one of the most fundamental laws of the Judean temple-state, the commandment not to work on the Sabbath (5:10-18). As becomes evident in Jesus' response, the rulers understand this commandment to be grounded in the order of creation. Exodus 20:11, in one of the versions of the Decalogue, forms the possible basis for their interpretation: the Sabbath should be observed carefully because God himself "rested the seventh day" after making heaven and earth. Jesus responds that insofar as his Father is still working, all the time, even on the Sabbath, he himself is also working (doing the work of giving life to the people, as in the healing). Another version of the Decalogue in the Pentateuch as we have it indicates a different understanding of the command to observe the Sabbath, probably what John's Jesus was working from. In Deut 5:13-15 observance of the Sabbath is grounded in God's deliverance of the people from hard labor in Egypt. In this version of Israelite tradition, which would clearly be in the interests of the villagers, the purpose of the Sabbath was to rest from heavy labor in order to restore life-energy — which would be directly to the point of the work of the Father that Jesus is doing, giving life to the people. But Jesus' reply only leads the Judean rulers to seek to kill him, both for breaking their law and for making himself equal to God.

Jesus' further reply places the Judean rulers in an impossible position. Not only does his life-giving work violate and supersede their law, but his Father has given all judgment to him (5:19-24). Moreover, as they presume to sit in judgment on him, not only do his works of life-giving and the Father testify on his behalf, but even their Scriptures (which *they* think give them eternal life) testify on his behalf. And he does not need to accuse them before the Father (the divine court), because Moses (giver of the law) is their accuser; indeed Moses wrote about him (vv. 31-47). Jesus is claiming that in his works he is displacing and replacing the whole temple-state apparatus. Indeed in rejecting and pointedly breaking their law, he co-opts it, claiming that the Scripture that the rulers claim as their authority is really about him.

At the festival of Booths/Tabernacles, Jesus resumes his attack on the law of the Judeans, which continues through the next several episodes, including the healing of the blind man, again in violation of the Sabbath (7:14–10:39). He presumes to teach in the temple, astonishing people because he is not literate, does not know "writing," the distinguishing mark of the professional scribal teachers, including the Pharisees (7:14-24). He accuses the Judean rulers of not keeping the law, in the sense of its logical, common sense implications. If the commandment to circumcise (only a part of a body) on the eighth day supersedes the commandment against working on the Sabbath, then how can they prosecute him for healing a whole person on the Sabbath? Concerned that his works are generating an increased following, the high priests and Pharisees send their servants to arrest him (vv. 32-52).

Continuing his attack on their law, specifically the requirement of two witnesses, Jesus claims to have the requisite two, himself and his Father, again simply rejecting and superseding their law (8:12-20); simultaneously he rejects and co-opts the Judean rulers' claim to have Abraham as their ancestor (8:31-59), and escapes from their attempt to stone him. After he forces the issue again with his second healing in violation of their Sabbath law, which evokes belief that he is a prophet, the Judean rulers resolve to expel from the assembly of the people anyone who confessed Jesus to be the Messiah (9:1-23). This brings to the fore the widening conflict between the disciples of Jesus and the rulers of the Judeans as "the disciples of Moses," who are seeking to kill Jesus as a sinner, that is, a (perpetual) lawbreaker.

Jesus' ensuing discourse about the sheepfold, the sheep, and the shepherd, versus the thieves and brigands who have preceded him, then makes clear what has been happening in all these episodes of conflict (10:1-18). The complex, extended metaphor, a traditional way of understanding a people and their leaders or rulers, is almost an allegory. The "sheepfold" is the new order of life for the people that Jesus is generating; the "sheep" are the people of Israel among whom he has been working;

the "gate" and the "shepherd" are Jesus himself, the one who lays down his life for the people and who grants them access to the renewed community. The "thieves/bandits/hirelings" who abandon the flock when the wolf comes are the Judean rulers, who have been plundering and killing the sheep. But this is the way that John's story has been representing the high priests and Pharisees, the rulers of the Judeans, throughout the series of conflicts over the healings on the Sabbath. They are the ostensible shepherds of the Israelite people, yet they are oppressive and the virtual agents of empire. They persecute people who bring life and interrogate people who have gained life (5:10-18; 9:13-34). They exile recalcitrant subjects (9:22) and pass death sentences against those who bring life to the people (5:18; 11:50; 12:10-11; 18:30-31). They dispatch strongmen to seize people who defy them (7:32, 45-52). And, as becomes vividly evident at the end of John's story, the Judean rulers are the local instruments of the Roman imperial order, acting in close collaboration with the imperial governor (18:28-31; 19:7, 21-22, 38-39) and publicly affirming their exclusive loyalty to Caesar against one of their own (19:12-15).

Messianic Demonstration

Just as John's portrayal of Jesus' mission of renewal begins with a prophetic demonstration against the rulers at the Judeans' festival of Passover, so it concludes with a messianic demonstration at the Judeans' festival of Passover. Jesus' entry into Jerusalem with the large crowd acclaiming him "the king of Israel" is his other major act of provocation against the rulers, this time more clearly against the Romans as well as the Judean rulers (as the latter state explicitly in 19:12). Like the prophetic demonstration against the temple, the messianic demonstration is paralleled in Mark (11:1-10), suggesting that the accounts depend on parallel memories of an event focused on Jesus at a Passover festival.

While Mark's account suggests the messianic character of the demonstration, John's story makes it explicit. Mark suggests Jesus' messianic pose in three ways, all subtle. In the second line of the followers' cry of "Hosanna," they acclaim "the coming kingdom of our ancestor David" (which is not a quotation of a prophecy or psalm, unless from popular tradition; Mark 11:10). Equally subtly, Mark has Jesus riding on a donkey (foal), evoking memory of a prophecy of Zechariah about how the liberating king would come to Zion as a humble king from among the people, riding a donkey rather than a war chariot (Mark 11:7-8; cf. Zech 9:9). Less subtly, in addition to the festal spreading of leafy branches on the path, Mark has Jesus' followers spreading their cloaks on the road before Jesus, a traditional gesture of acclaim and welcome for a liberating popular king (see especially the acclamation of Jehu, anointed by Elijah's protégé Elisha to lead the people against the oppressive monarchy under Ahab, 2 Kings 9). Matthew's account makes explicit what is implicit in Mark, including quotation of what the prophet Zechariah had "spoken" as fulfilled in this action. John's account is the most explicit of all. The crowd's Hosanna acclaims Jesus, "the one who comes in the name of the Lord," as "the king of Israel." The term "anointed" is not used, but we know from the outset of John's story that Jesus is the Messiah, the king of Israel.

John makes the quotation of what was "written" about the coming king sitting on a donkey's colt an afterthought: Jesus' disciples did not understand at first, but once he was "glorified" (crucified), then they "remembered" that these things had been written of him and done to him (12:15-16). Judging from the overall movement of John's story and especially the immediate context, in which the acclamation of Jesus as "the king of Israel" is followed by an indication of how he will be executed ("lifted up" on a cross), this citation of the Zechariah prophecy must be a confirmation that Jesus is a popular king, not an imperial king in a war chariot.

In John as well as in Mark, this messianic demonstration is the principal action of Jesus and his followers that suggests that he played (or was understood in) the role of a popularly acclaimed (anointed) king. Most of his other significant actions and the responses to them are fairly clearly, and often explicitly stated as, those of a popular prophet leading a movement of renewal, like Moses and Elijah. But both Mark and John give other indications that Jesus was understood in the role of a popularly acclaimed king. In John, after the feeding on the mountain, Jesus is afraid that the people will take him by force and make him king (6:15). Mark has Jesus sharply reject his acclamation as "Messiah" by Peter as well as the misunderstanding by James and John that he is or will become a king. There clearly appears to be a basis early in the response to and understanding of Jesus for John to have presented Jesus primarily as the Messiah, the king of Israel. And as we know from Josephus's accounts of the popularly acclaimed kings in 4 BCE and 67-70 CE, the title and role of popular king/anointed one was that of the leader of the renewal of Israel against the Roman imperial order in Palestine, including not only the Romans but also their Herodian and/or high priestly clients. Not surprisingly, then, in John's story it is the high priests and the Roman governor who collaborate to end Jesus' movement.

Why Jesus Was Crucified

The reasons for Jesus' execution have long been debated. The simple fact that he was crucified, a typical Roman punishment for rebel leaders, indicates that the Romans, not the Judean rulers, were responsible for his execution. But what had he done that would result in his crucifixion as "the king of the Judeans," the charge and the inscription on the cross?

The reasons for Jesus' arrest and execution have been unclear partly because they are somewhat unclear in Mark and the other Synoptics, which have been the sources used in study of the historical Jesus. Mark portrays Jesus performing healings and exorcisms primarily in the villages of Galilee. From a distance, his teachings and actions threaten the scribal authorities' social control, and he condemns the Pharisees' exploitation of the people to generate support for the temple. Not until the end, when Jesus goes to Jerusalem for a demonstration in the temple and to confront the high priests and scribes for oppression of the people, displaying an authority with the people that surpasses that of the rulers, does he seriously disrupt the public order that the Romans have charged the high priests with maintaining.

By contrast, John presents Jesus confronting the temple and the Judean rulers in Jerusalem virtually from the start and then again repeatedly throughout the story. From the outset, Jesus' renewal of Israel entails a rejection of the temple, and its festivals are replaced, for example, by a popular alternative celebration of Passover in the countryside. Jesus also directly confronts and rejects the official law/Scripture, of which the

Judean rulers (Pharisees) are the enforcers, as a controlling limitation on the people's life. While in Mark Jesus' movement of renewal is located mainly in the villages of Galilee and nearby areas, John has Jesus generating a movement in all the areas of Israelite heritage, but primarily in Judea itself. The expansion of this movement, as well as Jesus' attack on the temple and confrontations with the rulers increasingly threaten the Judean rulers' tenuous hold on power. After trying several times to arrest, stone, or kill Jesus, they finally formulate a plan to have him killed in order to keep the Romans from destroying the temple and removing them as incapable of maintaining order. The "trial" sequence communicates at every point that the high priests are dependent on the Romans, who have reserved for themselves the power of execution. The high priests carry out the typical role of a client elite, dutifully handing over an agitator who has become a threat to the imperial order. In John's Gospel, Jesus is crucified by the Romans because he has been generating a popular movement of renewal in opposition to the rulers of Judea and their Roman overlords.

The Gospel of John and the Jesus of History

―――――∽∾∾∾∽――――――

Although we have purposely narrowed our focus throughout this book to a reading of the Gospel of John as a story and its portrayal of Jesus' mission, this exploration may now provide a basis for brief consideration of the "spiritual" or "theological" aspects of the story and of John's story as a potential source for the historical Jesus.

Using John and Other Gospels
as Sources for the Historical Jesus

As noted in the Introduction, the Gospel of John has usually been taken as a source for the Christology and theology of the community that produced it, while text-fragments of the Synoptic tradition have been taken as the sources for the historical Jesus. This divergent deployment of the Gospels is firmly rooted in a combination of the theological orientation of New Testament studies and long-standing habits of reading the Gospels as (mere) collections of text-fragments such as sayings and pericopes.

In the last few decades, however, an increasing number of interpreters have recognized that the Gospels are sustained narratives in which the individual episodes are integral and inseparable components of a whole story, interspersed with speeches in which sayings are integral and inseparable components of those speeches. Research into aspects of the oral communications that dominated ancient societies, moreover, has strongly reinforced the recognition that the Gospels are stories, not mere containers. The Gospels were produced and performed orally in community settings, even after they had been inscribed on papyrus. And while recent text criticism is showing that particular sayings and other text-fragments may vary from manuscript to manuscript, studies of oral performance in traditional societies suggest that stories remain fairly consistent from performance to performance. Thus, not only are the Gospels whole stories that must be comprehended in their "literary" integrity, but also sustained stories that are relatively stable as historical sources, in contrast to text-fragments, which may have had no independent existence and function in communities of Jesus movements.

If the Gospels, including the Gospel of John, are all sustained narratives that offer plotted stories of Jesus and his mission, then John would appear to stand on the same ground as the Synoptics as a potential source for the historical Jesus. The recent revival of interest in John as a source for the historical Jesus,[1] however, has proceeded largely on the standard assumption that text fragments provide the "data" for scholarly reconstruction. The purpose of this book has been to explain that the Gospel of John is a story and to appreciate its portrayal of Jesus' mission. The implications for use of John as a source for the historical Jesus seem clear. Since John is a story, it can be used as a historical source only as a whole story, the episodes being understood as components of the story.

But how would we as historians move from the Gospel stories to the historical Jesus, whose interaction with the people and their rulers in the

---

1. For the revival of interest in the Gospel of John as a source for Jesus see Robert Fortna and Tom Thatcher, eds., *Jesus in Johannine Tradition* (Louisville: Westminster John Knox, 2001); Paul Anderson, Felix Just, and Tom Thatcher, eds., *John, Jesus, and History, Vol. I: Critical Appraisals of Critical Views* (Symposium Series 44; Atlanta: Society of Biblical Literature, 2007) and *Vol. II: Aspects of Historicity in the Fourth Gospel* (Early Christianity and Its Literature 2; Atlanta: Society of Biblical Literature, 2009). See also the discussion of the history of research, with proposals for future avenues of inquiry, in Paul Anderson, *The Fourth Gospel and the Quest for Jesus: Modern Foundations Reconsidered* (Library of New Testament Studies 321; London: T&T Clark, 2006).

historical context of Roman Palestine and Israelite tradition generated the movement(s) that produced the Gospel stories? Since interpreters of the historical Jesus have by and large been focused on text-fragments, not yet recognizing that the Gospels as whole stories are the sources, they have not addressed this key question. Clearly, much careful, critical, comprehensive consideration, including how texts-in-performance function, must be given to how the Gospels can be used as historical sources. But some of the requisite steps seem clear on the basis of the research in the areas discussed in the chapters above.

One is that the sources be evaluated for their independence of or dependence on one another. The consensus appears to be holding that Matthew and Luke were dependent on Mark, which seems to have been independent. Matthew and Luke also seem to have a common source of Jesus' speeches in "Q" (the "Sayings Source"), which is independent of Mark. John is thought to have known what a "gospel story" is, but to be a story independent of Mark's Gospel.

Another key step would be a comparison, in historical context, of the portrayals in the different Gospel stories, particularly those relatively independent of one another, for common features, variations on those features, and distinctive features. In the previous approach to the historical Jesus, scholars compared different versions of individual sayings to establish precious tidbits of "data" (whether Jesus may have uttered a particular saying). In sharp contrast, this comparison would look for indications of Jesus' main agenda, roles, interactions, and cultural patterns in the Gospel stories and component episodes and the speeches of Jesus that take very different forms (e.g., longer versus short narrative episodes [John versus Mark], short speeches versus long dialogues or discourses [Q versus John], speeches versus narrative episodes [Q versus Mark and John]), all taken in the broader context of the overall story or series of speeches. Such comparisons would lead to informed historical judgments regarding the more general features of Jesus-in-interaction-in-context, not to a list of aphorisms and other sayings that he presumably uttered. While other steps are pending, this step might be the most potentially suggestive and fruitful.

The basic plot and the broad portrayal of Jesus in both John's story and Mark's story have him catalyzing a renewal of Israel against the rulers of Israel, as laid out above. The series of speeches in Q present Jesus somewhat similarly, as engaged in the renewal of Israel while delivering oracles of judgment against the high priests and the (scribes and) Pharisees. This strongly suggests that the people involved in the communities that produced/cultivated John's story, Mark's story, and the Q speeches and/or their predecessors understood the renewal of Israel to have been Jesus' agenda. They also apparently viewed Jesus' death as a result of the conflict that this agenda inherently engendered between himself and the Roman and Judean authorities. This historical reconstruction of Jesus' mission in terms of the renewal of Israel against the rulers of Israel bears considerable credibility in a historical context where other known popular leaders and movements and even scribal protest movements held similar or parallel agendas.

The Gospel of John presents Jesus in the roles of both a popular prophet and a popular king/messiah. Mark's story presents him as a prophet like Moses and Elijah, but downplays and evidently rejects the response to Jesus as a popular messiah. The Q speeches have Jesus only in the role of a prophet, and know nothing of Jesus as a king. All three sources have Jesus acting and speaking and his followers responding to him in the role of a prophet leading a movement. But insofar as Mark's story, like John's, knows of Jesus understood as a popular king/messiah, and Paul, whose letters are dated to within two decades after Jesus' crucifixion, knows "Messiah/Christ" almost as if it were part of Jesus' name, Jesus must have been understood in the role of popular messiah/king very early. Josephus's histories indicate that both the prophetic and the messianic roles were deeply rooted in Israelite popular tradition and were so alive in the social memory of villagers at the time that popular movements took one or another of these social forms.

Both Mark and John present Jesus as a Galilean working initially in Galilee but then confronting the high priestly rulers in Jerusalem, in prophetic actions and pronouncements. As indicated in other sources, however, while Galilee had been under Jerusalem rule during the first century BCE, it was no longer under the political jurisdiction of the high priestly regime during Jesus' ministry. Recognition of the different regional histories of Galilee, Samaria, and Judea, particularly of the continuing effects of the earlier Jerusalem takeover and subjection of these other areas of Israelite heritage, may raise issues that were hidden by the standard scholarly construct of "Judaism."

Since Galilee had been ruled by Herod Antipas during the whole lifetime of Jesus, why did he not simply confront Antipas in Sepphoris, near Nazareth, or in Tiberias, not far from Capernaum, if he wanted to protest the rulers' exploitation of the people? Instead, Jesus confronted the rulers in Jerusalem, who did not have jurisdiction over Galilee at the time. The portrayal of Jesus as a prophet engaged in the renewal of Israel against the rulers in John, Mark, and the Q speeches may enable us to explain his focus on the Jerusalem rulers rather than Antipas. All three sources, John, Mark, and the Q speeches, agree that Jesus' mission was the renewal of Israel in the role of a prophet. Israelite tradition was rich in lore (stories, oracles) of prophets having pronounced prophecies and carried out symbolic actions against the rulers, mainly in Jerusalem. The role and agenda of a prophet in Israelite tradition that informed Jesus and his followers included confrontation of the rulers in the ruling city. And Jerusalem, which had been the ruling city of Israel in earlier tradition, had again been the ruling city of all areas of Israelite heritage for a hundred years prior to Jesus' lifetime.

After discerning the broader features of Jesus-in-movement by comparing the portrayals in the different Gospel sources, it might be possible also to investigate more particular aspects. But all these explorations must wait for more sustained projects of critical research and analysis.

The Spiritual Inseparable from the Political

As noted in the Introduction, in contrast to the standard view (since Clement of Alexandria) of the Gospel of John as a "spiritual" account, we have focused on the often underappreciated mundane aspects of John's story. If we now look again at the "spiritual" or "theological" aspects of the Gospel in the context of the story it presents, it is evident that they are inseparable from the political conflict of Jesus' renewal of Israel in opposition to the rulers in Jerusalem. Except perhaps for "the prologue," which starts with the spiritual ("the Word/Logos") and declares its incarnation in Jesus, the episodes of John's story start from particular actions of Jesus in opposition to the rulers and then articulate their meaning or spiritual dimension in dialogue and/or discourse.

Following Jesus' attack on the temple, John's story has Jesus pointedly travel through Samaria and speak to the woman at Jacob's well. As noted above, the episode builds on and resonates with both Judean and Samaritan social memory of the importance of the place in Israelite tradition and (implicitly) of the relatively recent conquest of Samaria and destruction of the Samaritans' temple by the Jerusalem high priests. This is the context of Jesus' declaration about worship of the Father in spirit and truth, which is inseparable from it. This declaration is not an abstract theological principle. The worship of God in spirit and truth is the new alternative to the politically-economically-culturally centralized celebration of festivals and performances of sacrifices in the Jerusalem temple (or the Samaritan temple). This is a *political*-religious declaration of independence from rulers and their centralized institutional base in temples.

John's story has Jesus again go up to Jerusalem for a festival of "the Judeans," where he purposely heals a crippled man on the Sabbath to provoke the rulers' enforcement of the law (5:1-24). This is the connection in which Jesus declares that his Father is working through his own work such as this healing and has given all judgment to the Son (who is being judged by the rulers). Jesus' declaration here explains why and how his renewal of the people rejects the official law, which is constraining for the people, limiting work that would generate life. Again it is not an abstract Christological statement but a political-economic declaration of independence of the people from centrally-determined political-religious law that places constraining limits on their lives.

The next episode in John's story opens with Jesus' feeding in the wilderness as a celebration of the exodus at Passover, including God's provision of manna, as a pointed alternative to the official Passover in Jerusalem (6:1-24). This is the context of his declaration, "I am the bread of life" (vv. 25-51). This "Christological" declaration, particularly the final specification that the bread that Jesus gives for the life of the world is his flesh (v. 51), is clearly a retrospective reflection on his crucifixion, his martyrdom for his cause of the renewal of Israel. Again, the statement is a political-religious declaration of independence of the people of Israel, specifically of the communities that have resulted from Jesus' mission as an alternative to the Roman imperial order in Judea, Galilee, and other areas.

Jesus' statement that he is the "good shepherd" who lays down his life for the sheep is again politically oppositional, against the Jerusalem rulers as thieves, bandits, and "hired hands" of the Roman imperial order (10:1-30). His declaration "I am the resurrection and the life" is an articulation of the healing of Lazarus that symbolizes his bringing renewed life to the people that evokes a new expansion of his growing movement that is threatening to the Jerusalem rulers and the Roman imperial order of which they are the guardians (11:1-53). This declaration also clearly comes from reflection on his having become a martyr to his own cause of renewal of the people. That indicates all the more clearly, however, that it is a politically revolutionary statement. Similarly the people's acclamation of Jesus as "the king of Israel" in response to his riding a donkey in fulfillment of Zechariah's prophecy of a popular king is a politically revolutionary cry — and again as recognized more clearly after reflection on his crucifixion as a rebel "king of the Judeans" (the Romans' view) to which it led (12:12-19, 32-33).

Strongly reinforcing the point that these declarations are not abstract Christological statements is Jesus' statement in the "farewell discourses" that "I am the way, the truth, and the life," so that "whoever has seen me has seen the Father" (14:1-14). While these declarations are typically viewed as prime evidence that the Gospel of John is a book of theological abstractions, when viewed in historical context Jesus' words point to a very different conclusion. If the people, the hearers of the Gospel story, focus on Jesus' works, on his mission of renewal of the people, including his martyrdom for having pursued that mission, they have seen God. So rather than look for God in theological statements, they should focus on Jesus' renewal of Israel in conflict with the rulers.

The "I am . . ." declarations in the Gospel, including the ones just mentioned, have been especially compelling text-fragments for Christological interpretation. These statements, along with the prominence of Jesus' discourses in John, have been the basis for the sense that the Gospel focuses everything in Jesus, the Messiah Son of God, often to the neglect of the community or movement of Christ-believers. Read as statements in John's story of Jesus' renewal of Israel, however, the "I am . . ." statements are not assertions about the nature of Christ in himself but thoroughly relational declarations that focus prominent symbols from Israelite tradition (social memory) in Jesus' actions so that they become life-giving for those who trust in (become loyal to) him.

The Samaritan woman articulates the expectation from Israelite tradition that "an anointed" figure is coming who will lead the renewal of the people so that worship of God will be in spirit and truth and no longer in a central temple headed by rulers. Jesus replies "I am" that anointed figure who is leading the renewal, a renewal that includes the Samaritans, many of whom became loyal to him (4:16-26, 39-42). In his interpretation of the broader significance of the wilderness feeding (central in the foundational exodus story), Jesus declares "I am" the living bread that gives life to whoever trusts in him, all of whom will be participants in the renewed people (6:25-39). Martha articulates the Israelite expectation of the future renewal of the people in which her brother Lazarus "will rise again in the resurrection on the last day." Jesus' declaration that "I am the resurrection and the life" brings this hoped-for resurrection-renewal from the remote future into the present in the raising of Lazarus, resulting in life for the Judeans who become loyalists in response (11:17-45). Finally, Jesus' declaration "I am the true vine," building on a long-standing extended metaphor for the people as God's vineyard (e.g., Isaiah 5), leads directly into its relational extension, "you are the branches," with the further explanation that the disciples will abide in him only if they bear fruit by keeping his commandment that they love (care for) one another, following his example of facing martyrdom for the movement (15:1-17).

Of course, one could, and many scholars do, abstract a "Christology" from these discourse components of John's sustained story of the renewal of Israel. But by attending to how Jesus identifies key symbols from Israelite tradition with his own work in his role as prophet/messiah bringing life to the people who join his movement we can appreciate how the broader meaning of his actions resonated with people deeply rooted in that tradition.

Works Cited

Achtemeier, Paul J. "*Omne verbum sonat:* The New Testament and the Oral Environment of Late Western Antiquity." *Journal of Biblical Literature* 109 (1990): 3-27.

Anderson, Paul. *The Fourth Gospel and the Quest for Jesus: Modern Foundations Reconsidered.* Library of New Testament Studies 321. London: T&T Clark, 2006.

Anderson, Paul, Felix Just, and Tom Thatcher, eds. *John, Jesus, and History, Vol. I: Critical Appraisals of Critical Views.* Symposium Series 44. Atlanta: Society of Biblical Literature, 2007.

————. *John, Jesus, and History, Vol. II: Aspects of Historicity in the Fourth Gospel.* Early Christianity and Its Literature 2. Atlanta: Society of Biblical Literature, 2009.

Asad, Talal. *Genealogies of Religion: Disciple and Reasons of Power in Christianity and Islam.* Baltimore: Johns Hopkins University Press, 1993.

Botha, Pieter. *Orality and Literacy in Early Christianity.* Biblical Performance Criticism. Eugene: Cascade, 2012.

Broshi, Magen. "The Role of the Temple in the Herodian Economy." *Journal of Jewish Studies* 38 (1987): 31-38.

Brown, Raymond. *The Gospel According to John.* 2 vols. Anchor Bible. New York: Doubleday, 1966/1970.

Carr, David. *Writing on the Tablet of the Heart: Origins of Scripture and Literature.* Oxford: Oxford University Press, 2005.

Charlesworth, James, ed. *The Messiah: Developments in Earliest Judaism and Christianity.* Minneapolis: Fortress, 1992.

Chatman, Seymour. *Story and Discourse: Narrative Structure in Fiction and Film.* Ithaca: Cornell University Press, 1978.

Clanchy, M. T. *From Memory to Written Record: England 1066-1307.* Cambridge: Harvard University Press, 1979.

Collins, John J. *The Scepter and the Star: Messianism in Light of the Dead Sea Scrolls.* 2nd ed. Grand Rapids: Eerdmans, 1995.

Crossan, John Dominic. *The Historical Jesus: The Life of a Mediterranean Jewish Peasant.* San Francisco: HarperCollins, 1991.

Culpepper, R. Alan. *Anatomy of the Fourth Gospel: A Study in Literary Design.* Philadelphia: Fortress, 1983.

Dagenais, John. *The Ethics of Reading in Manuscript Culture: Glossing the* Libro de buen amor. Princeton: Princeton University Press, 1994.

Dewey, Joanna. *Orality, Scribality, and the Gospel of Mark.* Biblical Performance Criticism. Eugene: Cascade, 2013.

Dodd, C. H. *Historical Tradition in the Fourth Gospel.* Cambridge: Cambridge University Press, 1963.

―――. *The Interpretation of the Fourth Gospel.* Cambridge: Cambridge University Press, 1953.

Ehrman, Bart. *The Orthodox Corruption of Scripture: The Effect of Early Christological Controversies on the Text of the New Testament.* Oxford: Oxford University Press, 1993.

Epp, Eldon. "The Multivalence of the Term 'Original Text' in New Testament Criticism." *Harvard Theological Review* 92 (1999): 245-81.

―――. "The Oxyrhynchus New Testament Papyri: 'Not without Honor Except in Their Own Hometown'?" *Journal of Biblical Literature* 123 (2004): 5-55.

―――. "The Significance of the Papyri for Determining the Nature of the New Testament Text in the Second Century: A Dynamic View of Textual Transmission." Pages 84-103 in *Gospel Traditions in the Second Century: Origins, Recensions, Text, and Transmission.* Ed. William L. Petersen. Christianity and Judaism in Antiquity 3. Notre Dame: Notre Dame University Press, 1990.

Eusebius. *The Ecclesiastical History.* Trans. Kirsopp Lake and J. E. L. Oulton. Loeb Classical Library. Cambridge: Harvard University Press, 1953.

Fiensy, David. *The Social History of Palestine in the Herodian Period: The Land Is Mine.* Lewiston: Mellen, 1991.

Foley, John Miles. *How to Read an Oral Poem.* Urbana and Chicago: University of Illinois Press, 2002.

―――. *Immanent Art: From Structure to Meaning in Traditional Oral Epic.* Bloomington: Indiana University Press, 1991.

―――. *The Singer of Tales in Performance.* Bloomington: Indiana University Press, 1995.

Forster, E. M. *Aspects of the Novel.* New York: Harcourt, Brace & World, 1954.

Fortna, Robert, and Tom Thatcher, eds. *Jesus in Johannine Tradition.* Louisville: Westminster John Knox, 2001.

Frei, Hans. *The Eclipse of Biblical Narrative: A Study in Eighteenth and Nineteenth Century Hermeneutics.* New Haven: Yale University Press, 1974.

Freyne, Sean. "Behind the Names Galileans, Samaritans, *Ioudaioi.*" Pages 39-56 in *Galilee through the Centuries: Confluence of Cultures.* Ed. Eric Meyers. Winona Lake: Eisenbrauns, 1999.

Goodman, Martin. "The First Jewish Revolt: Social Conflict and the Problem of Debt." In *Journal of Jewish Studies 33.1-2: Essays in Honor of Yigael Yadin.* Ed. Geza Vermes and Jacob Neusner. Oxford: Oxford Center for Postgraduate Hebrew Studies, 1982.

―――. *The Ruling Class of Judaea: The Origins of the Revolt Against Rome, A.D. 66-70.* Cambridge: Cambridge University Press, 1987.

Haines-Eitzen, Kim. *Guardians of Letters: Literacy, Power, and the Transmission of Early Christian Literature.* Oxford: Oxford University Press, 2000.

Halbwachs, Maurice. *On Collective Memory.* Ed. and trans. Lewis Coser. Chicago: University of Chicago Press, 1992.

Harris, William. *Ancient Literacy.* Cambridge: Harvard University Press, 1989.

Henderson, Ian. "*Didache* and Orality in Synoptic Comparison." *Journal of Biblical Literature* 111 (1992): 283-306.

Hengel, Martin. *Die Zeloten. Untersuchungen zur judischen Freiheitsbewegung in der Zeit von Herodes I. bis 70.* Leiden: Brill, 1961.

Hezser, Catherine. *Jewish Literacy in Roman Palestine.* Texts and Studies in Ancient Judaism 81. Tübingen: Mohr Siebeck, 2001.

Horsley, Richard. *Archaeology, History, and Society in Galilee: The Social Context of Jesus and the Rabbis.* Harrisburg: Trinity, 1996.

―――. *Galilee: History, Politics, People.* Valley Forge: Trinity, 1995.

―――. *Hearing the Whole Story: The Politics of Plot in Mark's Gospel.* Louisville: Westminster John Knox, 2001.

―――, ed. *Hidden Transcripts and the Arts of Resistance: Applying the Work of James C. Scott to Jesus and Paul.* Semeia Studies 48. Atlanta: Society of Biblical Literature, 2004.

————. "The High Priests and the Politics of Roman Palestine." *Journal for the Study of Judaism* 17 (1986): 23-55.

————. *Jesus and the Spiral of Violence: Popular Jewish Resistance in Roman Palestine.* San Francisco: Harper & Row, 1987.

————. *Jesus in Context: Power, People, and Performance.* Minneapolis: Fortress, 2008.

————. "Oral Communication, Oral Performance, and New Testament Interpretation." Pages 125-56 in *Method and Meaning: Essays on New Testament Interpretation in Honor of Harold W. Attridge.* Ed. Andrew B. McGowan and Kent Harold Richards. Resources for Biblical Study 67. Atlanta: Society of Biblical Literature, 2011.

————. *Performance in Text and Tradition.* Biblical Performance Criticism. Eugene: Cascade, 2013.

————. "Popular Messianic Movements Around the Time of Jesus." *Catholic Biblical Quarterly* 46 (1984): 471-93.

————. "Popular Prophetic Movements at the Time of Jesus, Their Principal Features and Social Origins." *Journal for the Study of the New Testament* 26 (1986): 3-27.

————. *The Prophet Jesus and the Renewal of Israel.* Grand Rapids: Eerdmans, 2012.

————. "Q and Jesus: Assumptions, Approaches, and Analyses." Pages 175-209 in *Early Christianity, Q, and Jesus.* Ed. John Kloppenborg and Leif Vaage. *Semeia* 55. Atlanta: Scholars, 1991.

————. *Revolt of the Scribes: Resistance and Apocalyptic Origins.* Minneapolis: Fortress, 2010.

————. *Scribes, Visionaries, and the Politics of Second Temple Judea.* Louisville: Westminster John Knox, 2007.

————. *Sociology and the Jesus Movement.* New York: Crossroad, 1989.

————. "The Zealots, Their Origin, Relationships, and Importance in the Jewish Revolt." *Novum Testamentum* 28 (1986): 159-92.

Horsley, Richard, and Jonathan A. Draper, *Whoever Hears You Hears Me: Prophets, Performance and Tradition in Q.* Harrisburg: Trinity, 1999.

Horsley, Richard, Jonathan Draper, and John Miles Foley, eds. *Performing the Gospel: Orality, Memory, and Mark.* Minneapolis: Fortress, 2006.

Horsley, Richard, and John Hanson. *Bandits, Prophets, and Messiahs: Popular Resistance Movements at the time of Jesus.* Harrisburg: Trinity, 1999.

Jaffee, Martin. *Torah in the Mouth: Writing and Oral Tradition in Palestinian Judaism, 200 BCE–400 CE.* Oxford: Oxford University Press, 2001.

Josephus. *Antiquities of the Jews*. Trans. Ralph Marcus and Allen Wikgren. Loeb Classical Library. Cambridge: Harvard University Press, 1963.

———. *Jewish War*. Trans. H. St. J. Thackeray. Loeb Classical Library. Cambridge: Harvard University Press, 1989.

———. *Life*. Trans. H. St. J. Thackeray. Loeb Classical Library. Cambridge: Harvard University Press, 1966.

Kelber, Werner. "Jesus and Tradition: Words in Time, Words in Space." Pages 139-67 in *Orality and Textuality in Early Christian Literature*. Ed. Joanna Dewey. Semeia Studies. Atlanta: Scholars, 1995.

———. *Mark's Story of* Jesus. Philadelphia: Fortress, 1979.

———. *The Oral and Written Gospel: The Hermeneutics of Speaking and Writing in the Synoptic Tradition, Mark, Paul, and Q*. Philadelphia: Fortress, 1983.

Kirk, Alan. *The Composition of the Sayings Source: Genre, Synchrony, and Wisdom Redaction in Q*. Leiden: Brill, 1998.

———. "Manuscript Tradition as Tertium Quid: Orality and Memory in Scribal Practice." Pages 215-34 in Thatcher, ed., *Jesus, the Voice, and the Text*.

Kirk, Alan, and Tom Thatcher, eds. *Memory, Tradition, and Text: Uses of the Past in Early Christianity*. Semeia Studies 52. Atlanta: Society of Biblical Literature, 2004.

Kloppenborg, John. *The Formation of Q: Trajectories in Ancient Wisdom Collections*. Studies in Antiquity and Christianity. Philadelphia: Fortress, 1987.

Kysar, Robert. *John: The Maverick Gospel*. 3rd ed. Louisville: Westminster John Knox, 2007.

Le Donne, Anthony, and Tom Thatcher, eds. *The Fourth Gospel in First Century Media Culture*. ESCO/LNTS 426. London: Continuum, 2011.

Lendon, J. E. *Empire of Honour: The Art of Government in the Roman World*. Oxford: Oxford University Press, 1997.

Lenski, Gerhard. *Power and Privilege: A Theory of Social Stratification*. New York: McGraw, 1966.

Malbon, Elizabeth Struthers. *In the Company of Jesus: Characterization in Mark's Gospel*. Louisville: Westminster John Knox, 2000.

Mason, Steve. *Flavius Josephus on the Pharisees: A Composition-Critical Study*. Leiden: Brill, 1991.

Mattern, Susan. *Rome and the Enemy: Imperial Strategy in the Principate*. Berkeley: University of California Press, 1999.

Moore, Stephen. *Literary Criticism and the Gospels: The Theoretical Challenge*. New Haven: Yale University Press, 1989.

Myers, Ched. *Binding the Strong Man: A Political Reading of Mark's Story of Jesus.* Maryknoll: Orbis, 1988.

Neusner, Jacob. *From Politics to Piety: The Emergence of Pharisaic Judaism.* Englewood Cliffs: Prentice-Hall, 1973.

Neusner, Jacob, William Scott Green, and Ernest Frerichs, eds. *Judaisms and Their Messiahs at the Turn of the Christian Era.* Cambridge: Cambridge University Press, 1988.

Nickelsberg, George W. E. *1 Enoch.* Vol. 1. Hermeneia. Minneapolis: Fortress, 2001.

Niditch, Susan. *Oral World and Written Word: Ancient Israelite Literature.* Louisville: Westminster John Knox, 1996.

Parker, David. *Codex Bezae: An Early Christian Manuscript and Its Text.* Cambridge: Cambridge University Press, 1992.

———. *The Living Text of the Gospels.* Cambridge: Cambridge University Press, 1997.

Reich, Ronny, and Eli Shukron. "The Siloam Pool in the Wake of Recent Discoveries." *New Studies on Jerusalem* 10 (2004): 137-39.

Rhoads, David, and Donald Michie. *Mark as Story: An Introduction to the Narrative of a Gospel.* Philadelphia: Fortress, 1982.

Richardson, Peter. *Herod: King of the Jews and Friend of the Romans.* Columbia: University of South Carolina Press, 1996.

Robinson, James, Paul Hoffmann, and John Kloppenborg, eds. *The Critical Edition of Q: Synopsis including the Gospels of Matthew and Luke, Mark and Thomas with English, German, and French translations of Q and Thomas.* Hermeneia. Minneapolis: Fortress, 2000.

Saldarini, Anthony J. *Pharisees, Scribes, and Sadducees in Palestinian Society.* Wilmington: Michael Glazier, 1988.

Sanders, E. P. *Jesus and Judaism.* Philadelphia: Fortress, 1985.

Scott, James C. *Domination and the Arts of Resistance: Hidden Transcripts.* New Haven: Yale University Press, 1991.

———. "Protest and Profanation: Agrarian Revolt and the Little Tradition." *Theory and Society* 4 (1977): 1-38, 211-46.

———. *Weapons of the Weak: Everyday Forms of Peasant Resistance.* New Haven: Yale University Press, 1985.

Segovia, Fernando. "The Journeys of the Word of God: A Reading of the Plot of the Fourth Gospel." Pages 27-45 in *The Fourth Gospel from a Literary Perspective.* Semeia 53. Ed. R. Alan Culpepper and Fernando Segovia. Atlanta: Scholars, 1991.

Shiner, Whitney. *Proclaiming the Gospel: First Century Performances of Mark*. Harrisburg: Trinity, 2003.

Small, Jocelyn Penny. *Wax Tablets of the Mind: Cognitive Studies of Memory and Literacy in Classical Antiquity*. New York: Routledge, 1997.

Smith, D. Moody Smith. *John*. Abingdon New Testament Commentaries. Nashville: Abingdon, 1999.

Smith, Morton. "Zealots and Sicarii: Their Origins and Relations." *Harvard Theological Review* 64 (1971): 1-19.

Tacitus. *Agricola*. Trans. M. Hutton and R. M. Ogilvie. Loeb Classical Library. Cambridge: Harvard University Press, 1980.

Thatcher, Tom. "Anatomies of the Fourth Gospel: Past, Present, and Future Probes." Pages 1-38 in *Anatomies of Narrative Criticism: The Past, Present, and Futures of the Fourth Gospel as Literature*. Ed. Tom Thatcher and Stephen Moore. Resources for Biblical Study 55. Atlanta: Society of Biblical Literature, 2008.

———. *Greater Than Caesar: Christology and Empire in the Fourth Gospel*. Minneapolis: Fortress, 2009.

———. *Jesus, the Voice, and the Text: Beyond the Oral and Written Gospel*. Waco: Baylor University Press, 2008.

———. *What We Have Heard from the Beginning: The Past, Present, and Future of Johannine Studies*. Waco: Baylor University Press, 2007.

———. *Why John Wrote a Gospel: Jesus–Memory–History*. Louisville: Westminster John Knox, 2006.

Ulrich, Eugene. *The Dead Sea Scrolls and the Origins of the Bible*. Grand Rapids: Eerdmans, 1999.

Van Belle, Gilbert. "The Faith of the Galileans." *Ephemerides theologicae lovanienses* 74 (1988): 27-44.

———. "The Prophetic Power of the Word of Jesus: A Study of John 4,43-54." In *Prophecy, Wisdom, and Spirit in the Johannine Literature*. Ed. B. Decharneux and Fabien Nobilio. Brussels: EME, 2013.

van der Watt, Jan. *An Introduction to the Johannine Gospel and Letters*. Approaches to Biblical Studies. New York: T&T Clark, 2007.

von Wahlde, Urban. "Archaeology and John's Gospel." Pages 523-86 in *Jesus and Archaeology*. Ed. James Charlesworth. Grand Rapids: Eerdmans, 2006.

———. *The Gospel and Letters of John*. 3 vols. Eerdmans Critical Commentary. Grand Rapids: Eerdmans, 2010.

———. "The Pool of Siloam: The Importance of the New Discoveries for Our Understanding of Ritual Immersion in Late Second Temple Judaism and the

Gospel of John." Pages 155-74 in *John, Jesus, and History, Vol. II: Aspects of Historicity in the Fourth* Gospel, ed. Anderson et al.

―――. "The Puzzling Pool of Bethesda." *Biblical Archaeology Review* 37.5 (September/October 2011): 40-46, 65.

Watts, James, ed. *Persia and Torah: The Theory of Imperial Authorization of the Pentateuch.* Symposium Series 17. Atlanta: Society of Biblical Literature, 2001.

Wire, Antoinette Clark. *The Case for Mark Composed in Performance.* Biblical Performance Criticism. Eugene: Cascade, 2011.

Wrede, Wilhelm. *The Messianic Secret.* 1901. Trans. J. C. G. Greig. Greenwood: Attic, 1971.

Yee, Gale. *Jewish Feasts and the Gospel of John.* Wilmington: Michael Glazier, 1989.

Zerubavel, Yael. *Recovered Roots: Collective Memory and the Making of Israeli National Tradition.* Chicago: University of Chicago Press, 1995.

Index